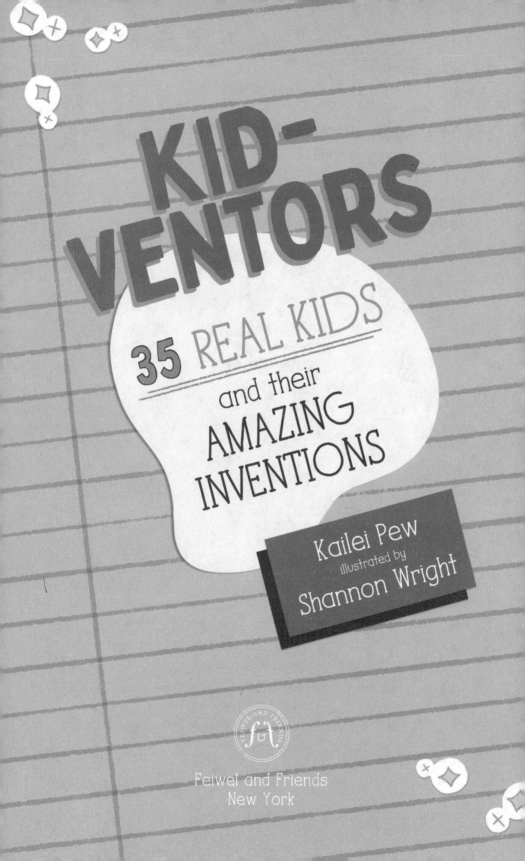

KID-VENTORS

35 REAL KIDS
and their
AMAZING INVENTIONS

Kailei Pew
illustrated by
Shannon Wright

Feiwel and Friends
New York

TO MY BROTHERS.

THE HOMEMADE GAMES, CAN-MOTORCYCLES, AND DUCT TAPE—
BUNGEE CORD CREATIONS MIGHT NOT HAVE BEEN AWARD-
WINNING INVENTIONS, BUT THEY WERE OURS.

AND THEY WERE WONDERFUL.

A Feiwel and Friends Book
An imprint of Macmillan Publishing Group, LLC
120 Broadway, New York, NY 10271 • mackids.com

Our books may be purchased in bulk for promotional, educational, or business use. Please
contact your local bookseller or the Macmillan Corporate and Premium Sales Department at
(800) 221–7945 ext. 5442 or by email at MacmillanSpecialMarkets@macmillan.com.

Library of Congress Cataloging-in-Publication Data

Names: Pew, Kailei, author. | Wright, Shannon (Illustrator), illustrator.
Title: Kid-ventors : 35 real kids and their amazing inventions / Kailei Pew ; illustrated by
   Shannon Wright.
Description: First edition. | New York : Feiwel and Friends, [2024] | Includes bibliographical
   references. | Audience: Ages 9–12 | Audience: Grades 4–6 | Summary: "From Popsicles and
   swim fins to robots and glitter shooting prosthetics, this middle grade nonfiction debut is
   full of fun and inspiring stories about real kid inventors and some of their most amazing
   inventions"— Provided by publisher.
Identifiers: LCCN 2023028096 | ISBN 9781250836021 (hardcover)
Subjects: LCSH: Children as inventors—Juvenile literature. | Inventions—Juvenile literature.
Classification: LCC T39 .P49 2024 | DDC 609.2—dc23/eng/20230630
LC record available at jttps://lccn.loc.gov/2023028096

First edition, 2024

Book design by L. Whitt

Feiwel and Friends logo designed by Filomena Tuosto

Printed in the United States of America by BVG, Fairfield, Pennsylvania

ISBN 978-1-250-83602-1 (hardcover)

1 3 5 7 9 10 8 6 4 2

I WANT TO BREAK THE STEREOTYPE THAT YOU HAVE
TO BE OLDER TO BE ABLE TO MAKE A BIG IMPACT
ON THE WORLD . . . NOTHING IS IMPOSSIBLE . . .
BE CURIOUS. DREAM BIG. NEVER GIVE UP.

—Prisha Shroff, sixteen-year-old inventor
of self-cleaning solar panels

CONTENTS

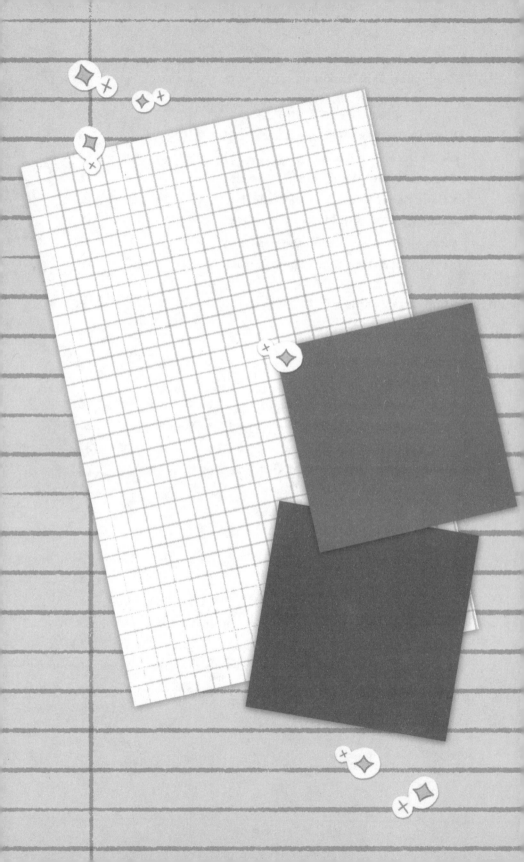

INTRODUCTION

Who do you think of when you hear the word "inventor"? An adult sitting alone in a lab testing idea after idea until—*eureka!*—the problem is solved? But what if I told you that some of the greatest inventions were dreamed up and made by *kids*? Swim fins, the windsurfer, and even Popsicles were all made by kids who figured out how to turn ordinary supplies into extraordinary inventions!

The thirty-five young inventors in this book are incredible. They asked questions and worked to find answers. They dreamed big and made important changes. Some of these kids came up with something completely new, and others built on, improved, or expanded existing ideas. Some worked for many months and even *years* to bring about their dreams, and others stumbled into the right answers fairly quickly. Some worked alone, and others looked to family, teachers, and mentors for guidance. But they all invented solutions to make the change they hoped for. No matter how hard the challenge.

When Remya Jose had to spend many hours washing her family's laundry by hand, she invented a pedal-powered washing machine so effective that she finished the chore in only twenty minutes! When Tripp Phillips's LEGO creations kept falling apart, he developed a glue strong enough to hold his creations together (even when dropped) but that would wash off when he was ready to build something new. And when Fatima Al Kaabi didn't have anyone willing to teach her about robotics, she turned to the internet to teach *herself* all the skills she needed—and created multiple crowd-pleasing robots in the process!

Have *you* ever dreamed of changing the world? Or even just a piece of it? You don't have to wait until you're an adult to come up with new ideas and make meaningful contributions! These thirty-five kid inventors sure didn't wait. They proved that even the youngest people can change the world.

INVENTIONS TO SOLVE DAILY PROBLEMS

A really good invention makes the world more awesome. Because the world is full of problems. But there's also lots of problem solvers!

—"Kid President," written by Brad Montague and portrayed by Robby Novak

BENJAMIN FRANKLIN

SWIM FINS

11 Years Old
Massachusetts,
United States
1717

Benjamin Franklin is probably one of the most famous inventors of all time. Throughout his life, he looked for solutions to everyday problems and ways to make life easier for himself and others. Bifocals, the Franklin stove, and the lightning rod are a few of his most well-known creations. Benjamin believed that his inventions were gifts, so he chose not to file for patents. Instead, he shared them with others for free. Maybe that's why so many people remember the inventions he made as an adult.

But what many people don't know is that Benjamin Franklin actually began inventing as a young boy. In fact, he created his first invention at only eleven years old!

Growing up in Boston, Benjamin loved the ocean. The water called to him, and he spent hours in the bay boating, exploring, and splashing in the waves. He especially loved to swim. And once he taught himself some

Benjamin: "We should be glad of an Opportunity to serve others by any Invention of ours; and this we should do freely and generously."

A LEGACY OF INVENTION

Benjamin Franklin is so well known and respected as an inventor that after his death, the Franklin Institute was founded in his name to promote science, invention, and technology.

basic strokes, he felt completely at home in the water. Still, he really wanted to swim faster.

Even as a kid, Benjamin understood Newton's principle that "for every action, there is an equal and opposite reaction." He knew that when he pushed water *behind* him with arm movements or flutter kicks, an equal force would push him *forward*. Thinking about this, Benjamin theorized that he could move more water, creating a greater force, by increasing the surface area of his hands (that is, by making them bigger).

First, Benjamin measured his own hands, grabbed some wood, and crafted two wooden ovals that extended well beyond his fingertips. But it was hard to hold on to the wood and swim at the same time. So Benjamin drilled a thumb hole into each oval. They ended up looking a lot like a painter's palette.

Benjamin took his new invention with him on his next swimming trip. He stuck his thumbs through the holes and squeezed against the boards. He dove in and used the wooden ovals to slice through the water and pull back with greater force. Benjamin paddled and kicked with all his might. His new gadget worked! He swam much faster with the wooden ovals in his hands.

But the palettes really hurt his wrists and Benjamin couldn't use them for long swims. Frustrated, he sat on the bank to think of a new solution. Eventually, he created a second prototype that strapped to his feet and fit like a pair of sandals. These paddles didn't hurt, and still worked to increase his speed. But he didn't love the way the hard wooden flippers hit the water and soon gave up on them. Still, even though they weren't everything he hoped they'd be, the swim fins stand as his first documented invention. Benjamin Franklin had begun a life of innovation.

The fins weren't Benjamin's only water invention. Or his only creation from childhood. Now that he'd figured out how to swim faster, Benjamin started thinking of ways to enjoy a *longer* swim without feeling exhausted by the end.

One day, soon after abandoning his swim fins, Benjamin spent the morning playing near a pond with a homemade kite. Soon he got hot, tied the kite to a stake on the bank, and plunged into the cool water. Floating along, Benjamin saw the kite drifting in the wind. Always curious, he wondered if he could swim and fly the kite at the same time.

Benjamin brought the toy into the water, floated on his back, and extended the kite into the air. When the wind caught the kite, it pulled him along in the breeze. How fun! And easy. Benjamin suddenly realized the kite might be the solution to his question of how to swim a longer distance.

Benjamin was so confident about his new idea that he asked a friend to take his clothes to the other side of the pond—about a mile away! At the time, it was common for boys to swim in only their underwear

FROM WOOD TO RUBBER

Imagine how awkward it would feel to have wood strapped to your feet while swimming. Since it's not flexible, the wood would slap against the water without any give. Luckily, today, swim fins are made from rubber and plastic so they can bend with the water.

THE KITE EXPERIMENT

Benjamin kept flying kites for the rest of his life. In fact, his most famous adult experiment involved one! Wanting to prove that lightning held electricity, Benjamin flew a kite with a metal key attached to it in a storm. Luckily, the kite was not struck by lightning—he probably would have been killed if it had been, so DON'T try this at home!—but, as Benjamin's kite flew into the storm, it picked up electricity from the surrounding lightning, which he felt from a small shock when he touched the key. He used this information and other experiments to develop his lightning rod a few years later.

instead of changing into special swimsuits. So, if Benjamin didn't make it across, he likely would have had quite the embarrassing walk back home. The friend agreed, and Benjamin went back to his kite.

Benjamin laid on his back in the water and found his balance. He sent the kite up into the air and let it catch the wind. It took a little while to adjust the kite—if it wasn't at the exact right height, it didn't work, and he stopped moving, but once he found a good altitude, he easily drifted across the pond, pulled entirely by the wind in the kite. It was some of the most fun he had ever had in the water. Even as a young boy, Benjamin had learned that he could invent a solution to almost any problem he encountered.

BENJAMIN WENT ON TO:

- Invent eight major devices used throughout the world
- Open the first public library in the United States
- Help draft the Declaration of Independence and the United States Constitution
- Appear on the first United States postal stamp

LOUIS BRAILLE
BRAILLE ALPHABET

Three-year-old Louis Braille spent a lot of time helping his dad in his leatherwork and saddle shop. Always happy, energetic, and curious, Louis brought a lot of good cheer into the workshop. He'd often chatter away while he watched his dad punch holes into the tough leather with sharp tools. He thought it looked like fun. So, one day, when his dad turned away for only a second, Louis tried to punch a hole himself. The tool slipped and plunged into his eye. His parents rushed him to a local healer, but it was too late. Louis lost his sight in that eye. Soon, infection spread to the other eye. He was completely blind by five years old.

The accident didn't change Louis's personality. He was still just as happy as ever. And he was determined to learn as much as possible, even though he couldn't see to read or write. At first, Louis studied at home. His dad hammered nails into a large board in the shape of each letter, and Louis memorized them by touch. His priest noticed how bright Louis was and offered private tutoring sessions. It didn't take long for the priest to realize that Louis's memory was so good that he held on to *everything* he was taught.

When Louis was seven years old, his priest encouraged him to

attend the neighborhood school. Louis worked hard to become one of the top students. But when the other boys read or wrote, Louis was left with nothing to do. He especially longed to read like the others. Knowing this, Louis's priest convinced a local leader to write to the Royal Institute for Blind Youth in Paris—a boarding school for blind children—requesting a scholarship for ten-year-old Louis. The institute agreed!

Attending the school would mean leaving his loving family for a group of strangers. It would mean trading his small town for a big city. But it would also mean an education he couldn't get anywhere else. Louis knew he had to go.

Life at the Royal Institute for Blind Youth was hard. The school director was mean. The building was dirty and cold. The students got sick a lot. There wasn't much food. And the children studied and worked for *fifteen hours* a day. But it was worth it to Louis. He finally had the chance to read.

The Royal Institute for Blind Youth had books with embossed, or raised, letters. Louis jumped into the new reading method, but it was slow going. He had to trace every individual letter with his finger and remember each one until he could create a word. And only a few sentences fit on a page, so the books were huge and hard to handle. It wasn't an ideal system, but it was all Louis had.

Louis: "To give blind people the ability to write, to allow them to surmount this obstacle that so markedly restricts their social relations is . . . a subject that should have been proposed for a prize by the various betterment societies; people will perhaps find I have made a contribution to solving this problem."

In 1821, two years after Louis started school, things started to get better when Dr. Alexandre-René Pignier took over as the director. The new leader made sure the students had enough to eat and tried to clean up the building. He even started looking for a better way to teach the children to read.

Dr. Pignier learned about a new "night writing" system created by Captain Charles Barbier de la Serre for the French army. Before then, soldiers had to light a candle or lamp to read messages from their leaders, giving away their position to enemy soldiers. But this new code could be read on a dark battlefield.

Though most of the students at the Royal Institute were boys, it's believed that a handful of girls also attended at this time.

The system used sets of twelve dots pressed into a thick paper with a stylus, or pointed stick. Each combination of dots represented one of the thirty-six phonetic sounds in the French language. Dr. Pignier hoped the system would work for his students, too, so he invited Captain Barbier to the school. The captain taught the children his new system, and it really worked! Louis was thrilled to find that he could read and even write much more easily.

SO MANY SOUNDS

"Phonetics" refers to the different sounds heard in speech. Each letter makes multiple sounds. Just read these words to see how many different sounds the letter "A" can make: apple, all, ape, any. Now you'll start to see how complicated the symbols were when based on phonetics.

But Captain Barbier's system wasn't everything Louis had hoped for. There were no symbols for punctuation, so it was hard to tell where one sentence ended and another began. It didn't have any symbols for numbers either, which felt pretty limiting. And since it was a phonetic system, there was no thought for proper spelling. Plus, it was still tricky to read. Using twelve dots meant that a reader needed multiple fingers to read a single symbol. Louis had some ideas for improvements. But when he asked Captain Barbier to consider the changes, the captain wasn't interested in taking ideas from a twelve-year-old boy.

So Louis decided to make the changes himself. He stayed up late into the night, long after the other boys in his dormitory had gone to bed, pressing dots into paper after paper. His goal was to invent a new language for the blind. The system needed to be easy to read and include marks for punctuation. Louis didn't like using two fingers to read a single sound. So he experimented with six dots instead of twelve, organized in two columns of three dots each. If it worked, each symbol could be felt by a single fingertip.

When school got out for the year, Louis still didn't have it worked out. He returned home and spent every moment of summer vacation

THINKING BACKWARD, UPSIDE DOWN

Louis used a stylus to push his dots into paper. For the letters to read correctly from left to right on the raised side, Louis had to press the dots into the back side of the paper from right to left and form the letters backward. Then, when he flipped the paper to the raised side, the dots were in the correct formation.

working on his ideas. But he couldn't get it right. He returned to school and again spent his nights making more and more dots.

Louis kept up this pattern for three long years. After only working with phonetic sounds, Louis finally realized he could focus instead on the alphabet. At fifteen years old, he created twenty-five unique symbols for each letter in the French alphabet. And it finally worked! He added more symbols for numbers, contractions, punctuation marks, and capital letters. He even went on to invent symbols for math and music.

Students at the Royal Institute for the Blind liked the new system right away. They were amazed at how easy it now was to read and write. But it didn't only change Louis's life or even just the lives of his friends. Braille, the system created by a fifteen-year-old boy, would go on to revolutionize reading and writing for the blind around the entire world.

LOUIS WENT ON TO:

- Teach at the National Institute of Blind Youth
- Publish a paper about how to use the Braille system
- Present at the Paris Exposition of Industry

KATHRYN "KK" GREGORY

WRISTIES

10 Years Old
Massachusetts,
United States
1994

One especially cold day, Kathryn "KK" Gregory shivered as she put the finishing touches on her snow fort. Her creation was impressive, but she was freezing. The gap between her gloves and coat exposed her skin to the frigid air, and snow had gotten into her sleeves. She wanted to play in the new fort, but her wrists were so wet and cold that she couldn't have much fun. KK trudged inside, trying to figure out how she could still enjoy the snow without feeling miserably chilled at the end of the day.

KK's mom suggested she sew something to solve her problem. So KK grabbed her family's sewing machine and a pile of fabric and got to work. She wrapped a strip of material around her wrist to make a loose cylinder design. Then she slid the fabric tube under the foot of the machine and slowly stitched a seam up the side. KK tried on the sleeve-like tube, but it didn't stay on. She cut a thumb hole into the design and put it on again. With her thumb poking through the hole, the cylinder stayed in place, covering her palm and wrist!

But would it keep her warm? KK sewed a second prototype to make a matching pair and got ready to brave the cold. She put her coat and gloves back on and slipped her new wrist warmers *over* her gloves and

under her coat sleeves. KK rushed outside to try out her new invention. At first, her wrist coverings provided the protection she hoped for. But soon, snow crept into the gap between her glove and the tube, and KK couldn't get it out. That was even worse than before!

Back inside, KK updated the design. She sewed a smaller cylinder that clung tightly to her palm, wrist, and forearm. Now the design fit snugly *under* both her gloves and coat. When she raised her arms, her coat sleeve slid down, but her skin stayed covered. And when KK tried her invention outside, the snow couldn't work its way into her glove or up her sleeve anymore. With only two prototypes, she had a working invention. She named the guards Wristies and decided to share them with her friends right away.

KK made a pair for each member of her Girl Scout troop. They loved the Wristies! With their stamp of approval, KK set out to sell her product—after all, other kids must have the same problem she did. But first, she needed to find a better fabric. After a few trials, she realized the material she had used on the first prototype got wet quickly, which was almost as bad as snow creeping in. KK needed something flexible, warm, and weather resistant. She and her mom tried different cloths and visited multiple stores until they found Polartec, a fleece fabric that checked all their boxes. Finally, they were ready to start production.

News about Wristies spread fast. But not everyone was complimentary. Some of the kids at school thought KK was weird for running a business. Others were jealous of the attention she got. And many didn't understand. They bullied KK and made fun of her Wristies. When things got especially hard to handle, KK reminded herself of all the good she was doing.

KK: "Goals have always been very helpful for me . . . Set them high, get there, and then make another one!"

By the time KK graduated from high school, she had managed the Wristies business—and the bullies—for eight years. And she was ready for a break. So she decided to go to college, travel the world, and focus on rock climbing while her mom took over the company, making sure that many more kids could stay warm while playing in the snow.

KK WENT ON TO:

- Appear on *Today* and *The Oprah Winfrey Show*
- Sell Wristies on QVC, becoming the youngest person at the time to sell on the show
- Become the youngest person ever nominated for the New England Entrepreneur of the Year Award (though she didn't win, her story inspired them to create a new award for young innovators the following year)
- Return to the Wristies business, partnering again with her mom, after eight years away
- Create new designs including Long Wristies, Short Wristies, Cuffed Wristies, and Heated Wristies

RICHIE STACHOWSKI
WATER TALKIE

Richie Stachowski had the experience of a lifetime at only eleven years old—a trip to Hawaii! You might think the culture, weather, and scenery wouldn't impact a kid as much as it might an adult. But Richie realized just how lucky he was. While snorkeling in the clear waters of the Pacific Ocean, he swam right alongside brightly colored fish, sprawling coral, and other gorgeous sea life. He had never seen anything like it!

As Richie paddled past each new creature, he wanted to talk to his dad about the amazing things he saw. But it was impossible to communicate under the water. Pointing and waving wasn't enough to express what he was feeling. Frustrated, Richie had to keep his excitement to himself.

On the drive back to the hotel, Richie asked his dad if there was any way to talk underwater. His dad did some quick research and found there wasn't anything like Richie was envisioning. Though some earlier inventions had tried to solve the problem, none had really succeeded. They ended up not working, only working in very specific situations, or being way too expensive for a regular person to afford. Richie set out to change that. He sketched his first ideas in the hotel room that very night.

Once he returned home from vacation, Richie got serious about his invention. He researched underwater acoustics, or the way sound moves through water. Richie learned that sound actually travels faster and farther through the water than it does through the air. But the sound is muffled and distorted because people aren't used to being—or hearing—underwater. Richie's challenge would be to create a device that could make the words come out *clearly*.

Richie read books and went swimming as much as possible to understand more about sound in water. When he tried to talk while submerged, he made too many bubbles. Those bubbles masked the sound of his words, making it hard to understand anything he said. Everything just sounded like "blub, blub, blub." Richie needed to come up with a way to project the sound forward while minimizing the bubbles.

Richie bought supplies and started trying out new ideas. First, he took the mouthpiece off a snorkel. Then he cut the cone off a soccer field marker. He put the two pieces together to make a megaphone-like device. Richie headed to the pool to test the prototype. Unfortunately, it didn't work the way he envisioned.

GLUB, GLUB, GLUB.
WHY CAN'T WE HEAR UNDERWATER?

Sound travels about four times faster through water than air. But sound waves coming through the air vibrate off the bones in our inner ear, making it simple to hear. Underwater, the waves don't start vibrating until they get to the skull bone. This is because our bodies are mostly made of water. Our fleshy ears are so similar to the water surrounding them that the sound waves pass right through.

Water rushed through the cone and into Richie's mouth. On top of that, holding a snorkel mouthpiece in place made it impossible for Richie to move his lips. He couldn't speak clearly at all with his teeth clamped around the plastic. But if he didn't keep his lips closed, he choked on the water. And he was still making way too many bubbles when he spoke. Richie needed more supplies. He gathered his entire life savings, all $267, to buy new materials.

Richie worked for a month making adjustments and trying new prototypes. To tackle the issue of flooding, he needed to make the device airtight. Since wrapping his lips around the mouthpiece like a snorkel hadn't worked, he used an elastic-like plastic to create a suction cup that fit firmly around *the outside* of his lips. He took a deep breath and sealed the plastic over his mouth before going underwater. It worked much better, with only a bit of water getting through the front.

Richie: "If you think you have a good idea, just go for it!"

Richie added a thin plastic cover to the large cone end of his invention to *completely* stop the water from entering. This membrane also helped create vibration and send the sound waves out into the water. Win-win! But he *still* needed to stop bubbles from coming out when he talked.

Richie added one-way blow valves to the sides of his invention. The air that came in the cone when he spoke now left through the sides. He even used a special valve that only made tiny bubbles. They were so small, and aimed in a different direction, that they didn't block the sound of his words from moving forward!

Richie took his newest prototype to the pool, pressed it over his lips, and dove under the water. He started talking and could actually understand himself! His family members and friends helped him test this final prototype and realized they could clearly hear each other through the water from up to fifteen feet away! Richie named his new invention the Water Talkie and never missed a chance to talk underwater again.

RICHIE WENT ON TO:

- Sell Water Talkies in Toys"R"Us, a major toy retailer of the day, as well as in Walmarts and Kmarts across the United States
- Invent two other water toys, the Scuba Scope and the Bumper Jumper Water Pumper
- Create his own company and eventually sell it to Wild Planet Toys

KAROLI HINDRIKS
FASHIONABLE REFLECTORS

16 years old
Pärnu, Estonia
1999

Growing up in Estonia under the rule of the Soviet Union, Karoli Hindriks didn't have many freedoms. Travel wasn't allowed. No one could own a private business. And even if they had wanted to, there weren't extra goods to sell. But the people resisted. And when Karoli was eight years old, she watched the big tanks leave her town. Slowly, freedom, light, and hope returned. Karoli especially loved seeing Estonian people open their own businesses, invent new gadgets, and build a better world. She wanted to be part of that.

The chance came years later when Karoli started thinking about the *physical* darkness in Estonia. The country is so far north that in the winter, the sun doesn't shine for eighteen to twenty hours a day! So, to stay safe, anyone walking had to wear reflective strips on their clothes. Karoli understood the need for the reflectors—she didn't want to be hit by a car because she couldn't be seen. But she felt like a traffic cone while wearing them.

When she was sixteen years old, Karoli's friends chose her to lead their class in a new assignment. They were supposed to develop a new business idea, and they wanted Karoli to act as the president of their

TECHNOLOGY BLOOMS IN ESTONIA

Today, Estonia is considered a major technology hub in the world. After the Soviet departure, so many people began inventing—and the independent government invested so much into technology—that the advancements skyrocketed. Now there are more start-up businesses per person in Estonia than in any other place in the world, and almost everything in the country is done digitally.

company. She felt surprised and a little overwhelmed, but excited that her friends thought she was a good leader.

Karoli remembered the inventors and shop owners in her own neighborhood who had brought so much light to her family after the Soviet occupation. She still wanted to be like them. And this was her chance.

Karoli and her friends brainstormed some ideas as a group. They thought of everything from selling funny T-shirts to making a new kind of lunch box. But nothing stuck.

One day after school, Karoli thought again about the ugly reflectors she had to wear. Was there any way she could improve the way they looked? Nothing came to her at first. But when she took her backpack off, she saw a teddy bear key chain dangling from one of the zippers and inspiration struck. Maybe she could make a reflector that was as cute as the bear! She drew up a few ideas for reflective necklaces with drawn-on animals, then shared the concept with her class the next day. Everyone agreed to work on the cool, kid-friendly update.

Karoli sketched more detailed plans for her new invention and got to work on the first prototypes. She cut out circles of fabric, just larger than a bike reflector, and tried to sew them together to make the necklaces. But when the samples came out super wonky, she realized she was terrible at sewing. Luckily, some of her classmates were much better at crafts. They took over the sewing, and the necklaces turned out great!

Karoli and her team drew animals and other patterns on each piece, then punched a hole in the top of the design and ran a thread through the hole to make the necklace. Finally, Karoli cut apart her ugly reflective strips and glued them around the circles. For an early design, the necklaces looked amazing! But would they work?

Karoli tested the necklaces by shining a light on them in the dark. The light bounced off the reflectors and shined right back to Karoli. She knew they would show drivers where the kids were walking. She shared a few prototypes with friends and waited for their feedback.

The kids loved the fashionable design and were glad to throw out the ugly strips they had worn before. Karoli and her classmates built

DARK DAYS AT THE POLES

At the North and South Poles, the sun doesn't shine during the winter because Earth's axis tilts them away from the sun. Areas close to the poles will have the same phenomenon, so some cities in northern Norway, for example, stay dark all day with only about an hour of slight light. As you move farther from the poles, the sun shines more and more. Estonia has a few hours of light each day during the winter, but the sun doesn't rise until after 9:00 a.m. and will already be setting around 3:00 p.m.

The opposite of this phenomenon happens in the summer months, with the sun always shining.

their business model and began sharing the necklaces. But pretty soon, they faced another issue. The reflective material that Karoli had glued on didn't stay put. At the end of one rainy day, all the safety strips had fallen off. The necklaces still looked good, but if they couldn't protect the kids from oncoming traffic, then it wasn't worth it.

Karoli went back to the drawing board. She searched for a reflective fabric to make her necklaces all out of one piece. Eventually, she found exactly what she needed from the company 3M. She ordered their reflective material, and her friends got to work sewing another batch of necklaces. This time, they drew the cute designs directly onto the reflective material and sewed them onto felt backs. Now there was nothing to fall off. Karoli shared the new prototype with classmates and hoped for the best.

This time, the necklaces were just right, reflecting light from passing cars without coming undone. Her team finished their project and presented it to the class. Their teacher loved it, and the team got great feedback. But Karoli wanted to help kids beyond her own classroom. She wanted to get her reflective necklaces throughout *all* of Estonia.

When Karoli shared her goal with her parents, they jumped on board. Her dad encouraged her to visit the local patent office to see how much it would cost to protect the new invention. Karoli agreed to at least ask, even though she didn't think she could afford the process. But when she got to the office, she got a big surprise. An attorney overheard her sharing her idea and was impressed. He had never met a kid inventor before and was so excited about Karoli's work that he offered to complete the patent application pro bono—for free!

Karoli became the first person under eighteen years old to get a patent in Estonia. It was such a big deal that the Minister of

Economy—one of the top government officials in the country—came to give her the certificate. That was really cool, but Karoli didn't care as much about all the recognition. She wanted her invention to help others.

Karoli started by cold-calling businesses throughout the country to see if they would stock her necklaces. She flipped through the phone book (this was before the internet really took off) and found company names she recognized. Some agreed to a meeting, and some even wanted to sell her reflectors in their stores. But getting the product to them was a big obstacle.

Karoli's family car was old and run-down. And in the winter months when the temperatures plummeted, it didn't start at all. So Karoli packed up her reflectors and took trains and buses all across Estonia, trying to deliver her products to different stores. It was hard and took a really long time. Finally, one day, while enjoying tea with her dad, an idea came to her. What if she asked a car company to let her use a car in return for free advertising?

Karoli: "There are solutions to all hard situations—we just have to be bold enough to see them."

Karoli made a list of the five car dealers in her area. She met with the first one, but they turned her down quickly. So did the second. And the third. And the fourth. Karoli worried she had dreamed too big. She knew she only needed one "yes," but it was hard to hold on to hope after so many rejections. Still, she had one last company to ask—Citroën. If they also said no, she could always keep using public transportation. But she'd never know until she tried.

So Karoli met with Citroën. She pitched her idea and crossed her fingers. After taking her last chance, Karoli couldn't believe their response—they actually wanted to help. And they didn't just give her an old model that no one wanted anymore. They gave her a *brand-new* car to use for her deliveries! To show her gratitude, Karoli put a reflective banner on the side of the car, advertising that Citroën supported traffic safety.

With such a huge success under her belt, Karoli realized other companies might be willing to help get her reflectors to kids all over Estonia. So she decided to ask gas stations to donate fuel for her deliveries. And this time, it only took two tries. Dio, a locally owned station, said yes and donated gas for two full years.

Karoli loaded the reflectors into her new car, filled up the tank, and started across the country. Now she could deliver her product without delay. Kids loved how cute the necklaces were, and parents loved how easy it was to convince their kids to wear them. Thanks to Karoli's vision, persistence, and dedication, thousands of kids started using the reflectors to stay safe—and look great while doing it.

KAROLI WENT ON TO:

- Become the CEO of MTV Estonia
- Appear multiple times on the TEDx stage
- Start an international business–Jobbatical–to get professionals into different countries where their skills were needed
- Be featured in *Forbes* and *Business Insider* magazines

CASSIDY GOLDSTEIN
CRAYON HOLDERS

11 Years Old
New York,
United States
1999

Cassidy Goldstein wanted to color beautiful pictures that she could display on the fridge. She wanted her teachers to praise her work. She wanted to feel proud of her art. But she struggled with fine motor skills. Things like holding a pencil, fastening a button, or anything else that used the small muscles in her hands were hard for Cassidy. That meant drawing didn't come easily to her.

Cassidy's parents called in a tutor to help. On the first day of lessons, the tutor asked her to draw a landscape to see what she could do. But when Cassidy gathered her supplies, she only had broken crayons that were extra hard for her to hold on to. The drawing didn't come out well and Cassidy became frustrated. The tutor understood and didn't force her to finish. She gave Cassidy the whole week to work on the project, which she would check at the next lesson.

But even with the extra time, Cassidy couldn't hold on to the short crayons. Still, she was determined to do the assignment. She searched around the house and found twelve small plastic tubes left over from a bouquet of roses. The tubes had been on the ends of the rose stems and had been filled with water to keep the flowers fresh for shipping.

Cassidy looked at a tube's opening and figured it was about the same width as her crayons, but much longer. She stuck her broken crayons into the tubes and discovered a great way to keep coloring. The tubes were big enough that Cassidy could grasp them more easily. And the crayons fit snugly without falling out. Without much effort, she had invented a basic crayon holder.

When Cassidy's tutor came to the next lesson, she was shocked. Cassidy's drawing was beautiful. Her tutor couldn't believe she had done it. Previous drawings hadn't been nearly as good because of Cassidy's fine motor difficulties. When Cassidy showed off her invention, her tutor was thrilled. She thought the simple idea was a stroke of genius. The tutor took half the crayon holders (even though Cassidy wanted to keep them all) and showed them to other teachers and therapists in the area.

Sometimes the best place to start with a new invention is to use something that already exists and repurpose it to do something new.

The phone started ringing off the hook. Teachers wanted the crayon holders for their students and asked where they could buy a set. Cassidy's dad, Norm, knew a lot about sharing a new product. He had a number of patents himself and had sold some of his

PATENT REQUIREMENTS
You don't have to have a physical prototype to file for a patent in most countries, but you do need a clear explanation of the invention and good drawings to show how it would work.

Within a patent application, inventors reference similar patents and then give a detailed description on how theirs is different.

own inventions. So he offered to help get the crayon holders to the public. Cassidy liked the idea, but she needed to create her own original prototype, not just use the flower tubes, before she could go any further.

Cassidy studied the tubes and used the idea from that first prototype to create her own design. She drew up an idea for a wide plastic tube that held tightly to crayons, pastels, or chalk so that kids could easily grip their coloring utensils. Once she finished, she wanted to get a patent so her invention would be protected.

Cassidy and Norm hired a patent attorney. He warned them that the process would be difficult. He couldn't guarantee they would get the patent in the end. In fact, he was pretty certain they would be denied. But Cassidy was determined to help other kids like her. She worked with the attorney to finish the application. Then they waited.

Their request *was* rejected. The patent office said the design wasn't unique enough. But Cassidy wouldn't give up. She worked with the attorney to study similar patents. Many other holders used friction to hold the writing utensils. This meant the crayons or chalk had to be forced into the tubes with plenty of pressure. They were hard for kids to use, and the crayons would often break from the force. Other patented crayon holders had lots of small pieces, making

Cassidy: "Kids are 25 percent of our population, but 100 percent of our future . . . we are the generation of tomorrow, so why not throw our ideas out there today?"

them dangerous for young kids. Still others were made with expensive materials, making the final product too pricey for kids to buy.

After the first denial, Cassidy applied again, telling the patent office how her product was different from the others. Her tubes let the crayons slide in easily. They didn't use any small parts. And they were made with an affordable plastic. But again, she was denied. She tried to reword her application another time to convince them, but that didn't work either.

So Cassidy decided to make a change to her prototype. She added a button that opened and closed the holder so that the crayon slid in and out more smoothly while keeping an even tighter grip once it was closed, no matter how narrow the writing utensil. Cassidy submitted her fourth application, including the details on the new button, and hoped this time would be different.

And it was! Finally, three years after inventing her crayon holder, Cassidy received a patent for her creation. With Norm's experience in manufacturing and production, he helped Cassidy find a company to make a mold for the crayon holder. Then they partnered with a licensing company that got the product into stores.

Cassidy's crayon holders sold in packs of two, with her story printed on the back. Now her invention could help kids everywhere hold on to their crayons, create beautiful works of art, and know that they could invent just like she had.

CASSIDY WENT ON TO:

- Share her invention on television and in the newspaper
- Be named the first ever national youth inventor of the year by the Intellectual Property Owners Education Foundation
- Co-found By Kids For Kids (BKFK) with her dad to help kids invent and get patents
- Create an "Inventive Thinking Toolkit" to teach kid inventors
- Make enough from selling crayon holders to pay for all four years of college

SOFIA OVERTON
WISEPOCKET SOCKS

11 Years Old
Arkansas, United States
2017

Sofia Overton was always on the go. She bounced from school to sports practice to a friend's house, leaving her parents guessing where to find her. So they bought Sofia her first cell phone. It came with very specific rules. It wasn't for playing games, scrolling social media, or browsing the internet. Instead, she was *supposed* to use it to call her parents in between the different activities so they would know where she was at all times.

But checking in wasn't as easy as it seemed. Sofia's pockets were never big enough to hold her cell phone, so she usually forgot to bring it along. Her parents were not happy, always wondering where she was, and Sofia was sick of getting in trouble. But she didn't have an easy way to carry her phone.

When Sofia saw her cousin carrying a phone in her boot, it seemed like a good solution. So Sofia decided to try it and slid her own cell phone into her boot. But the phone bounced around her ankle, making it harder to walk. Not to mention how tricky it was to fish the phone out. The whole thing was really annoying. Sofia knew there had to be a better way.

Once Sofia sat down to think about it, an idea came to her: socks

with a pocket big enough to hold a cell phone in place. She grabbed a pair of long socks and sewed a pocket onto the outside using extra-wide ribbon. Sofia put the socks on and slipped her cell phone into the outer pocket, just below her knee. She walked around to test the invention and realized that it wouldn't work. The cell phone either flopped out of the pocket or the entire sock sagged.

So Sofia tried the same idea, but with different material for the pocket. That prototype still didn't work. She tried many different fabrics, sewing pockets onto the outside of the sock, but none of them kept the phone in place. Frustrated, Sofia asked herself why the pockets weren't working. She realized that the different fabrics used for her pockets didn't have the same stretch as a sock.

Suddenly, Sofia had a breakthrough—what if she cut the top off a sock and sewed it *inside* another sock? That way, the pocket would stretch and move with the sock, and the phone would stay right next to her leg, hopefully unable to fall out. She got two pairs of socks and sewed them together as she had imagined—creating a pocket on the *interior*. Once again, she slipped her phone into place. She walked around. She ran. She jumped up and down. And . . . the sock actually worked! The phone stayed in place and out of the way. Finally, she had her first working prototype!

Sofia knew the design was good and shared it with her friends and classmates. Some of them worried that the phone would be in the way, or that the weight would make the socks slip down. But when Sofia convinced them to try the new socks, the kids were shocked. They stayed up, even with the extra weight from the phone. In fact, the design was so sleek that they hardly noticed the phone at all. They all agreed: The socks were great.

Then Sofia met kids who needed to carry things like EpiPens, insulin, and inhalers. Before, those kids had to wear fanny packs or special bags filled with their medical supplies—drawing unwanted attention. But with Sofia's socks, they could carry the items under the radar. Now that she knew her socks were good for more than just holding cell phones, she wanted to get them out into the market.

Sofia named her creation WisePocket Socks for the "wisely placed" pocket. Armed with a great name, she commissioned a logo to go with it. After all, she knew a cool look was the key to gaining attention. Her team created an owl design to match the "wise" name, and Sofia felt like it was just right.

With the product, the name, and the logo in place, Sofia was ready to market her invention. But to get her socks into mass production, meet minimum order requirements, and get a design patent, she needed at least $10,000!

So Sofia launched a crowdfunding campaign with the goal to raise the funds in one month. She made a cool video and uploaded it to the fundraising platform. She shared the page with her friends and followers. And she watched the donations come in. The campaign was an "all or nothing" fundraiser. If she didn't get enough pledges, she wouldn't see any of the money. And after three weeks of promotion, she was only halfway to her goal.

Sofia tried not to panic, but she couldn't help worrying. During

IT'S ALL ABOUT THE NUMBERS

A minimum order requirement is the smallest number of a product that a manufacturer agrees to make. Manufacturers often set a high minimum order to ensure they make enough money.

the last week of the campaign, she made even more social media posts. She filmed extra videos. She pleaded for new supporters to join the cause. She even offered bigger incentives to backers. And the donations increased—but it still wasn't enough. On the last day of the fundraiser, Sofia's heart fell. With only *nine hours* left to meet the goal, she still needed $900 in pledges.

Sofia turned to social media to make one final plea. She watched the fundraiser counter slowly rise. Would she make it? As the campaign ended, Sofia crossed her fingers and logged on one last time. With only seconds left, she hit $10,006 in pledges. She could finally breathe a sigh of relief, with just six dollars to spare . . . talk about cutting it close! Sofia thanked her backers, placed her first bulk order, and prepared to get WisePocket Socks out into the world. No one—including Sofia—would need to worry about leaving their phone behind again.

Sofia: "I've gotten this far with the help of my awesome parents, business mentors, and amazing community."

SOFIA WENT ON TO:

- Receive a design patent
- Donate a pair of socks to a child in need for every pair of WisePocket Socks sold
- Appear on *Shark Tank* and receive a $35,000 investment
- Send socks to all fifty US states
- Design new styles of socks and pocketed leggings

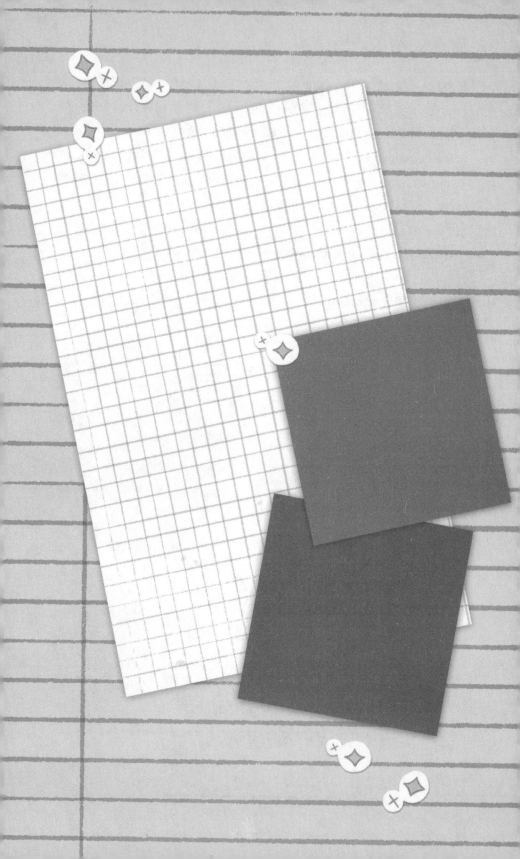

PATENTS AND TRADEMARKS

Patents protect inventors' work by preventing others from stealing both their ideas and often many years of work. The patents themselves tell a remarkable story of human ingenuity and serve a greater public good by preserving knowledge.

-Dr. Temple Grandin

You'll read a *lot* about patents and trademarks in this book. But what exactly are they? What do they do? Do you need one for every invention? How do you even get one? Let's take a look.

WHAT IS A PATENT?

A patent is a legal right or license, given by a government, to protect new and unique inventions. By getting a patent, you register that *you* are the inventor, and no one else can make, use, or sell your patented invention without your permission. And if they try, you can sue them.

Patents are public knowledge. Anyone can read your patent, and each patent is so detailed that other people could easily re-create your invention once the patent expires.

HOW LONG DOES A PATENT LAST?

Well, patents aren't good forever. Just look at the trampoline. At first, George Nissen was the only person who could legally make trampolines. But once his patent expired, *anyone* could use his original idea. And now you see trampolines being made all over the place.

But don't worry. Patents are good for a long time. Long enough for you to get a good jump on the competition. In many countries, patents are good for up to twenty years if they are maintained by paying yearly fees. But be careful—even if you are granted a patent, if you don't pay that fee, then you might lose your rights.

HOW DO YOU GET A PATENT?

Getting a patent isn't easy. In fact, it's downright difficult. First, you have to file an application with the patent office of a specific country or region. Applicants must describe their invention in great detail, prove that the idea doesn't already exist in another patent, and show that the invention isn't something that people could think up using only common sense.

An invention has to be unique in order to qualify for a patent, but it doesn't have to be a *completely* new idea. In fact, most recent patents are improvements on existing inventions. New applications must reference previous patents that are in the same vein and then explain why their invention is different enough for its own patent. But the quickest way to be denied is if the patent office doesn't think your idea is unique *enough*.

It's so tricky to write out the application that most inventors hire a patent attorney to help with the complicated process. But, of course, that makes things even more expensive. You have to pay for the attorney, the filing fees, and the maintenance fees . . . In all, you will probably need more than $20,000 to get the patent. Yikes!

And that's only if you file in just one country, because there's no such thing as an international patent. If you want your invention protected throughout the world, you have to register for a patent in *every country* where you want the protection. Luckily, more than 150 countries have joined The International Patent System, which lets inventors seek protection in multiple countries with just one application. But inventors still have to pay the fees and translate the patent into each language of the country where they want to hold one.

TYPES OF PATENTS

Every country offers multiple types of patents. It can be hard to understand because each country has their own system. It's especially tricky when different countries use the same name for very different types of patents! (Do you see why people usually hire a lawyer to help with this process?) Here are a few of the most common:

- **Invention patents** (called **utility patents** in the United States, **standard patents** in Australia, and simply **patents** in some countries) are the most common type of patent. They protect new inventions that have been proved useful and unique. Unless otherwise noted, this is the type of patent you will read about in this book.

- Have you ever heard of the phrase "patent pending"? Some countries offer **provisional patents** as a buffer while an inventor finalizes their invention or completes the long application process on a full invention patent. Others let inventors use the "patent pending" label without having to file anything else.

- **Design patents** protect new, unique designs and the looks of already existing inventions. Some places, like the United Kingdom, don't require a formal patent to protect designs. Instead, they have laws that automatically protect designs for a certain number of years with options to formally register later.

- **Utility models** (not to be confused with utility patents) are available in some countries, but not in the United States, United Kingdom, or Canada. It's easier to get a utility model. Plus, they aren't as expensive and don't need as much maintenance. But they also offer less protection for a shorter amount of time, though the details vary from country to country. These are often used for rapidly changing areas of invention, like technology, where you don't need protection for a full twenty years (just look at things like cell phones—a new model will be out almost every year).

DO YOU NEED A PATENT?

Well . . . that depends. If you've finished your invention and are thinking of getting a patent, ask yourself:

- What do I want to do with my invention?
  If you only want to use it yourself or share it with family and friends, you probably don't need a patent. If you want to mass produce, market, and sell your new creation, you will likely want one.
- Where do I need protection for my invention?
  If you only plan to market it in your home country, getting a patent from your local patent office will be enough. If you want to share your invention with a wider audience, you'll need a patent in each country where you plan to share it.
- How will I pay for the patent?
  Remember, patents can cost up to $20,000 in filing and maintenance fees, attorney fees, and more. Is that worth it to you? If yes, consider creating a fundraising campaign, finding sponsors, or connecting with an organization that helps young inventors.
- Do I want the details of my invention to be shared with the world?
  Remember, once your patent expires or you stop paying maintenance fees, you will no longer have a monopoly. That can actually be a really great thing! Patents help people learn and build upon existing inventions. Sharing that

knowledge brings progress. But it's not for everyone. Some inventions rely on trade secrets instead, keeping the details of a product within a small group who sign nondisclosure agreements (or promises not to tell). Other inventors who avoid receiving a patent get trademarks instead to protect their brand.

WHAT IS A TRADEMARK?

A trademark is a legally protected name, logo, word, phrase, or other recognizable symbol—even unique colors can be trademarked! If you have a trademark, no one else can use it on their product without your permission.

HOW DO YOU GET A TRADEMARK?

You can get a trademark by filing an application with the patent and trademark or intellectual property office. But before you can register, you first have to make sure that no one already has a similar trademark. Then you apply and pay the right fees.

But you can only get a trademark if you're going to use it on goods or services. So part of the application process includes detailed proof that you either have sold your product or will sell it in the near future. The trademark process is shorter and cheaper than the patent application process. Even with legal fees, registered trademarks only cost about $1,000.

HOW LONG DOES A TRADEMARK LAST?

Unlike patents, trademarks can theoretically last forever. Once you get approval, you will have the exclusive right to use your trademark on your product for as long as you maintain the trademark by paying the right fees. Every country has different rules for how often you have to pay to maintain the trademark, so make sure to check in your area.

TYPES OF TRADEMARKS

Registered trademarks are what we've been talking about so far; trademarks that are approved and recognized by the government. Registered trademarks offer the most protection and can use the ® symbol to show their status.

- **Standard character trademarks** are words, numbers, letters, or a mix of the three—without a particular design—to protect the *name* of a product. Examples of companies that hold this type of trademark include Coca-Cola, Adidas, and Walmart.
- **Special form** trademarks include the design, color, and/or style to protect the *look* of a product. Examples include the golden-arch-M in the McDonald's logo, the colors and font of the Google logo, and the swoosh of the Nike logo. Special form trademarks are often attached to company names with standard character trademarks.

Unregistered trademarks haven't been registered with a government office. They aren't as strong as registered trademarks, but still have some protections under common law (understood through custom or court rulings rather than written law). Unregistered trademarks can use the trademark label: ™. An unregistered trademark is only protected in the geographical region where you do business. This is sort of tricky to understand, so let's look at an example. If you opened a shop in Phoenix, Arizona, and started selling a new and original kind of hat that you name CoolHedz™, no one else in Phoenix could use the name CoolHedz in their business. But if someone in New York City started selling a new kind of Bluetooth headphone and called it CoolHedz, you wouldn't have any rights to the name there, unless you received a *registered* trademark good throughout the United States.

WHEN TO GET A REGISTERED TRADEMARK

To decide if you need a registered trademark, ask yourself:

- Do I plan to sell or market my invention?
  If not, you don't need—and in fact can't even get—a trademark.
- Do I care if anyone else uses the same name on a different product?
  Remember that if you don't have a registered trademark on your product name, nothing stops people from using the word/logo in another place.
- Will I sell the product nationally or locally?
  If you plan to sell locally, you will be fine without a registered trademark and can use an unregistered trademark to cover your product in your area. If you plan to sell nationally, you will need to register to fully protect the trademark.

A QUICK WARNING

If you do decide to file for a patent or register a trademark, remember: The government isn't going to check whether someone is using your invention or product name and tell them to stop. That responsibility falls to *you*, the patent or trademark holder. If you find out that someone is using your invention or trademarked name without permission, it's up to *you* to do something about it.

First, you can talk to the person using your work. Sometimes people just don't know, and they're using your stuff by accident. Talking to them might be enough to get them to change. But if they refuse to stop, you might have to take them to court and get a judge involved. Doing so can be messy and expensive (those pesky attorney fees again), so hopefully it never comes to that.

INVENTIONS TO HELP OTHERS

My biggest drive to be an inventor is my desire to help people and solve problems. It's very rewarding for me to see that I can improve the life of someone else.

–Mark Leschinsky, eight-year-old inventor of a self-disinfecting hazmat suit

SPENCER WHALE
KIDKARE RIDE TOYS

6 Years Old
Pennsylvania,
United States
1998

Spencer Whale *needed* to be an inventor. It was all he could think about since his brother, Brandon, had invented an improvement to his mom's pacemaker that helped send her heart data to the hospital. For that invention, Brandon became the youngest ever inductee into the National Gallery for America's Young Inventors at only eight years old.

Still in preschool, Spencer wasn't old enough to apply yet. But he watched his brother make a difference with his inventions and knew that he wanted to do the same.

When he finally got to kindergarten, Spencer prepared to follow in Brandon's footsteps. Unfortunately, he didn't have an idea for an invention. He just knew he wanted to help kids his age. And after watching his mom go through so many heart procedures, he thought there was probably something he could do for patients in the hospital. Spencer's mom got permission for them to visit the local children's hospital. They walked around and talked to the patients.

Spencer noticed that the kids who received medicine through an IV didn't get to play in the same ways the other kids did. Those

HONORING KID INVENTORS

The National Gallery for America's Young Inventors honors up to six new inductees every year. Kindergarteners through twelfth graders can apply or be nominated for consideration. The honorees are chosen by a panel of high school students with some guidance from an adult board.

without IVs rode toy cars through the halls. But the kids with IV poles had to either stay in bed or risk running over the tubes and pulling out their needles.

Spencer watched them trying to enjoy the cars while their parents or nurses pushed the IV poles behind them. They couldn't go as fast as the other kids. The IV tubing often got stuck in the wheels of the cars. And the kids didn't have any independence, relying on caregivers while they played. But the kids couldn't go without their IVs. They needed that medicine.

Spencer: "Most young people (myself included) need serious help discovering what they truly care about and how they can make a difference in the world."

Spencer realized that if he could attach the IV pole to the car, then the tubes wouldn't drag behind or get caught in the wheels. And the kids would be able to play on their own. After drawing up the idea, he wanted to craft a prototype.

But he didn't have enough money to buy a toy car. And he didn't have an IV pole.

But Spencer didn't give up. He found a contest called Student Ideas for a Better America that didn't require a physical model. He entered his sketches, crossing his fingers to win enough money to make his idea into a real invention. And he won! With the $100 prize money, Spencer was ready to buy the materials to make a prototype.

Before he could do it though, he got a big surprise. The owner of Step2 (a manufacturer of toddler toys) had seen an article about Spencer's idea. He loved it and donated toy pedal cars to the project. The children's hospital found some broken IV poles to donate as well.

With supplies in hand, Spencer continued working on ideas, sketching plans in a logbook, and recording the process. For every step, he took a picture and wrote about what he had done—at least as well as a six-year-old could write, misspelled words and all.

Spencer's two biggest challenges were (1) finding a way to attach the poles, while (2) keeping the cars balanced once the poles were added. He started by simply tying the poles onto the cars. He knew it wasn't a long-term solution, but it helped to visualize his idea. Then he could see if the IV pole was too heavy. When it was, the car tipped over. Spencer added counterweights in the front of some models to keep all four wheels on the ground.

Now Spencer needed to attach the poles permanently. Unfortunately, he didn't have the skills to do that himself. Neither did anyone in his family. But his grandma knew some people who did. She

PUMPING FLUIDS

IV stands for "intravenous," meaning "in the vein." An IV tube sends medicine, blood, or other fluids directly into a patient's vein. An IV tube is put in with a needle and can stay in place for about three days before needing to be switched out for a new one. A pole holds the bags of liquid and the pump that sends medicine into a patient's veins.

A SUREFIRE CONNECTION

Welding attaches pieces of metal together by heating the pieces until they begin to melt and then hammering them together and letting them cool as one.

connected Spencer with local mechanics who donated their time to the project. They welded the poles onto the cars, carefully following Spencer's instructions.

The prototype *seemed* ready. But Spencer felt it was a bit dull. So he added decorative, colorful tape to the poles. He hoped the bright colors would make kids smile, even while they went through difficult treatments in the hospital.

Spencer named his invention KidKare Ride Toys. He donated six cars to the local children's hospital where they received them happily. Spencer visited soon after, anxious to see if his invention really worked. His tests had worked at home, but none of them used real medicine on the IV poles. This would be the first time that kids who used IVs got to try the cars.

As Spencer walked the halls, he couldn't help but smile. Kids squealed as they pedaled along—completely on their own. Even as they rounded corners, the IV poles stayed firmly attached! And the tubing stayed safely off the floor without tugging on the needles. Nothing tipped over, parents didn't worry about their kids yanking out their IVs, and kids loved the cars!

Spencer's cars worked so well that word about the invention spread. A hospital in New York called him and asked for their own set of Kid-Kare Ride Toys! They brought Spencer out and gave him the materials he needed and a team to work with. Soon, kids were zooming through the halls of Winthrop-University Hospital, IV poles safely attached.

It turned out that helping other kids was more than enough for Spencer. He was proud of the work he had done, regardless of the recognition. Still, it *was* nice when he got his wish. At just six years old, Spencer was inducted into the National Gallery for America's Young Inventors, replacing his brother as the youngest ever inductee. But Brandon wasn't mad. He was glad he inspired his little brother to make a difference through invention.

SPENCER WENT ON TO:

- Get a patent for his invention and a license deal with a major toy company
- Travel the United States to give inspirational speeches and teach other kids about the invention process
- Keep inventing throughout his youth until choosing to focus on theater after high school

REMYA JOSE
PEDAL-POWERED WASHING MACHINE

14 Years Old
Kerala, India
2003

Remya Jose and her twin sister weren't happy about their new chore. Doing the entire family's laundry had always been their mother's job, but after she got sick, the task fell to the girls. Every week, they lugged piles of dirty clothes to the river. They pounded out stains with rocks. They scrubbed and lathered the clothes with soap. They rinsed them in the cold water and wrung them out to dry. All by hand. The task took *hours*, taking them away from their schoolwork and other activities.

While Remya washed each piece of clothing one at a time, she dreamed of an electric washing machine that could wash an entire load at once. But it was out of the question. The machines were very expensive. Her family couldn't afford such a luxury. And even if they could, electricity wasn't reliable in their town.

Remya had competed in science fairs before and knew she had a talent for mechanics. She realized she could use those skills to make her own washing machine—one that used mechanical energy instead of electricity. Maybe something she could crank and spin with her arms.

Remya studied electric washing machines to learn how they

THE ENERGY OF MOTION

Mechanical energy is the power created when energy is transferred in motion, like with a hammer hitting a nail, wind spinning a turbine, or a person pedaling a bike.

worked. The clothes were placed in a big drum. Hoses and tubes filled the drum with water. People added soap and started the wash cycle. A part in the middle (called an agitator) mixed and spun the clothes to get them clean. The soapy water drained from the drum and fresh water poured in to rinse the clothes. A final spin removed extra water.

Remya thought the electric process was simple enough. But the drum was very heavy when filled with the clothes and water. Remya knew that her arms weren't strong enough to spin something like that. But her legs might be able to handle the weight. Maybe she could invent a pedal-powered machine.

Remya shared her idea with her parents. At first, they discouraged her. They didn't understand the concept. And even worse, her dad thought she *should* only be washing by hand. He argued that someday she would get married, and young brides (he felt) needed to know traditional homemaking skills.

Remya didn't understand why her dad wouldn't support her. His outdated opinions hurt. But Remya knew he was wrong. She rejected his ideas and persisted with her invention.

Remya sketched ideas for a mechanical washing machine. She took everything she had learned about the electric machines and used it in her drawings. Once Remya finished her design, she showed her parents again. This time, with the plans in front of them, they could finally visualize it. Her dad apologized for doubting her and became her biggest supporter. He bought the supplies she needed and talked with a local car shop about welding the pieces together.

Remya visited the auto shop to talk about her ideas. She shared her sketches and worked closely with the mechanics to make sure they understood her design. Together they created an aluminum box with a rotating mesh cylinder to hold the clothes inside. The holes would let water get through to the clothes. Remya ran a metal bar through the cylinder and out of two openings on the sides of the box. She attached bike pedals to the bar so that when she pedaled, it would spin the inner container. The clothes would also beat against the bar, helping with the cleaning process.

Once the mechanics helped Remya finish her prototype, it was time to test the invention. She filled the box with water and detergent. She added the clothes to the barrel. She let them soak for ten minutes. Then she pulled up a stool and put her feet on the pedals. She took a deep breath and cycled. After five minutes, she opened the drain on the side of the box and let the dirty water run out. Then she added clean water to the box and pedaled again. After this rinse cycle, she opened the drain one more time. A final speed-round of pedaling removed the excess water. Her legs had been strong enough to complete the load! But had it worked?

THE CENTRIFUGAL EFFECT

When things move in a fast circle, they push away from the center. (That's why you can swing an open bag in a circle over your head without the contents falling out.) In Remya's final speed cycle, the extra water pushed toward the edges of the cylinder, through the mesh holes, and into the outer box, leaving the clothes mostly dry inside.

Remya crossed her fingers and took the clothes out of the washer. She looked them over. She smelled them. She grinned in victory. The clothes were clean! And they were even almost dry. When Remya had washed the clothes in the river, she had never been able to wring all the water out, and had needed to hang dry them, making the already time-consuming job even longer. But now she had clean and almost dry clothes in about twenty minutes. Much better! And best of all, Remya was able to help her family without losing the time for her studies.

Remya: "Whatever you have in mind, try it. Don't worry about making mistakes, they can surely be corrected."

REMYA WENT ON TO:

- Receive a patent
- Win the National Award from Abdul Kalam, the President of India
- Appear on The Discovery Channel with her invention
- Update her invention (as an adult) with a seat attached directly to the machine

LILY BORN
KANGAROO CUP

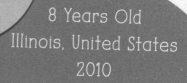

Lily Born had a great relationship with her grandpa. He told the best stories and could always make her laugh. But when she was seven years old, Lily noticed that his Parkinson's disease made it hard for him to use a cup. His shaky hands caused lots of spills. Lily's grandpa was embarrassed, and her grandma was constantly cleaning the messes.

Lily watched closely and realized that holding the cup wasn't the problem. The spills happened when her grandpa tried to pick the cup up or set it down. His tremors made it hard to get a steady grip, and the cup often tipped before he could lift it. Or when he tried to set it down, the cup slipped again, and some liquid sloshed over the side.

Lily decided to invent a cup that wouldn't tip over. She experimented with her own body, trying to figure what keeps something balanced. She asked her friends and family to push her over again and again. When she stood with her legs close together, she fell after each shove. But if she spread her legs far apart, she stayed standing. Lily imagined that she'd be even sturdier with a third leg to provide counterbalance. Maybe a cup with multiple legs would be better balanced too.

Lily drew up designs for a cup with three legs spaced far apart. She crafted the first prototype using moldable plastic. She created a circular ring with three legs that slid onto an existing cup. Lily put a regular cup into her invention and pushed. It slid across the table but didn't tip!

Parkinson's disease causes shaking that starts in the hands and can progress to the whole body.

Lily's grandpa tried the prototype. He slowly reached for the cup, lifted it from the table, drank, and set it back down. All without spills! He loved the cup and used it every day. Lily had solved her grandpa's problem. She named her invention the Kangaroo Cup after kangaroos who use their tail as a third leg.

A year later, Lily's dad spilled coffee across his computer. He tried to save it, but liquids and electronics don't mix well, and there was no hope for the keyboard. Lily realized that her grandpa wasn't the only one with a spilling problem. But the ring she'd made her grandpa wouldn't fit onto a coffee mug. Maybe Lily could use the same three-legged idea to create an entire cup.

So Lily's aunt took her to a local pottery studio. Lily learned about wheel throwing, or shaping pottery on a spinning wheel. It was tricky. She had to put the clay in the exact center of the wheel,

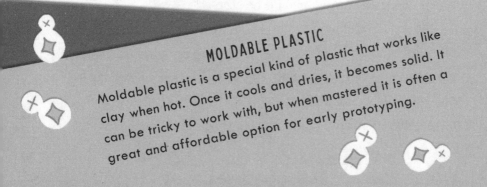

MOLDABLE PLASTIC

Moldable plastic is a special kind of plastic that works like clay when hot. Once it cools and dries, it becomes solid. It can be tricky to work with, but when mastered it is often a great and affordable option for early prototyping.

or it would fly off. And she couldn't jump into making a complicated three-legged cup. She had to start with the basics.

At first, Lily crafted lumpy bowls and plates. But in time, as she learned good techniques, her pottery got smoother. After many months, Lily made a ceramic cup on the wheel. She formed three ceramic legs and attached them to the base. Her teacher put the whole thing in the kiln until it hardened. She carefully pulled it from the heat to reveal the first all-in-one version of the Kangaroo Cup. This prototype had a lot of promise. It still had a few lumps, but it worked even better than the first cup holder. And since it was ceramic, it could hold hot or cold drinks.

Lily gave the new Kangaroo Cup to her dad. He loved it. And his computer was safe. After using it every day for some time, he realized how fantastic the Kangaroo Cup really was. He asked Lily if she wanted to mass produce and sell her invention. She knew it would be a lot of hard work, but she wanted to try.

Together, Lily and her dad worked to craft an even smoother model. With her dad's experienced hands, the new prototype didn't have even the small lumps. With this third prototype ready, they traveled to China, where Lily's dad had a friend in the ceramic business, to submit their new design for mass production. At the time, Lily didn't realize what a big deal this was. The trip cost more than her dad's broken-down car! But he believed in Lily and the Kangaroo Cup so much that he invested in the idea.

Lily and her dad spent two weeks in their friend's pottery studio, learning the ins and outs of mass-producing ceramics. It wouldn't make sense to craft every single cup by hand. That would take way too long. Instead, Lily and her dad visited the studio every day, helping the workers create a mold that could be used over and over again.

Lily had to make a few adjustments so that the cup could come out of the mold easily. Her final design still had three sturdy legs. It also curved in slightly toward the top so that liquid wouldn't slosh out under a shaky hand. Lily crafted a few cups in China and returned home ready to share her invention with others. After running a fundraising campaign, she placed a larger order for more than three hundred cups. But she faced some delays when the cups got stuck in customs after arriving from China. Some of her customers were impatient, but most were kind and understanding.

Soon, Lily's family weren't the only ones to love the Kangaroo Cup. But even after two years of designs and updates, the cup still had some drawbacks. The ceramic cup was breakable, so parents didn't want their kids using it. The handles were so wide that it was sometimes hard to hold. And water got trapped in small crevices, making it hard to dry the cup out.

Lily: "Just because you're a kid doesn't mean you can't do big and great things."

Now ten years old, Lily knew she wanted a plastic version of the Kangaroo Cup, but complicated plastic designs required an expertise that she didn't have. She realized she needed a design team. Luckily, Lily found a great group who had the skills to solve the problem, while still keeping her very

MAKING IT THROUGH CUSTOMS

The United States Customs and Border Protection agency (often just called "Customs") taxes and approves the import and export of goods into and out of a country.

A UNIFORM PRODUCT

Injection molding is a great option for mass production because it makes a uniform product every time. The process sends melted plastic into a mold where it cools and hardens. The original mold is expensive, but after the upfront cost, each individual product is cheaply produced. For large enough orders, it becomes an affordable option.

involved in the process. They chose to make the cup using injection molding. Once Lily raised enough money for the mold, the cups could be made cheaply in huge batches. After two years of working toward this new version, Lily was ready to see the final results.

The new cups were everything Lily wanted—unbreakable, sleek, and comfortable. Even more orders came in for the plastic version. Thanks to Lily and her team, the Kangaroo Cup could solve spilling problems from adults *and* kids all over the world.

LILY WENT ON TO:

- Share her story with kids all over the United States
- Create an Inventor's Workbook to help others design and craft their own ideas
- Appear on television and in the news
- Be named a CNN Hero for her work on the Kangaroo Cup

MARIA VITÓRIA VALOTO
LACTOSE-REMOVING CAPSULES

16 Years Old
Paraná, Brazil
2015

When Maria Vitória Valoto was ten years old, her whole life turned upside down. She had to move away from her hometown, leaving behind all her friends. The move was necessary. Her mom was going through cancer treatments and her family needed to be near relatives who would help support her. But it was still difficult, and sadly, her mom passed away soon after.

Full of grief, and in an unfamiliar place, Maria Vitória threw herself into her schoolwork—science especially—to cope with the loss. Four years later, her biology teacher, recognizing her focus and talent, told her she was good enough to get into global science fairs if she could come up with the right project. It all sounded so glamorous to Maria Vitória—a chance to travel the world, meet kids who were as interested in science as she was, and present her inventions. She especially hoped to attend the Google Science Fair. No Latin American student had ever made it before. And she was determined to be the first.

But Maria Vitória didn't just want the glamour. She wanted a project that could truly make a difference. As she brainstormed who she might help, she thought about her dad, who was lactose intolerant. He hadn't enjoyed a milk product for many years. In Brazil,

lactose-free dairy products and pills to ease the symptoms were so expensive that he couldn't afford them.

But some people with lactose intolerance, like young children, didn't have the choice to simply give up dairy. They needed the nutrients. So many families struggled with the costs of lactose-free products.

Maria Vitória studied the pills that some people took to ease the symptoms of the condition. When they took the pills after eating dairy products, they didn't seem to have bad reactions. Maria Vitória theorized that she could use the same concept but put whatever was in the pills directly into the milk to stop the problem at the source.

Maria Vitória's teacher loved the idea. But her school's lab didn't have the right equipment for such a huge project. Her teacher reached out to the local university to ask for lab time. Luckily, the university had a group of master's students working on milk projects. They liked Maria Vitória's idea and invited her to join their research team. Together they began crafting capsules to be put directly into a pitcher of milk, hoping to remove the lactose completely. They used the same ingredients found in the pills, especially beta-galactosidase, a molecule that helps people digest milk products.

But at the university, Maria Vitória sometimes felt out of place. The rest of the team had undergraduate degrees. They understood proper scientific procedures. But Maria Vitória was only fourteen years old

TUMMY TROUBLES

Lactose intolerance is the inability to digest the sugar found in milk products. If someone with the condition eats lactose, they'll be in store for a major bellyache, gas, and even diarrhea.

and had never done such formal scientific work. One day in the lab, she added the prototype from the day before to a new pitcher of milk. She hadn't realized she wasn't supposed to reuse the capsules. When the team saw what she had done, they explained why she shouldn't have reused the old prototype—they needed to keep everything exactly the same from one experiment to the next. But when Maria Vitória tested the milk, she discovered that the used capsules still worked!

What had seemed to be a mistake proved to be a breakthrough. If consumers could reuse the capsules, their cost would be even lower! So Maria Vitória and the team began adding the capsules to multiple containers of milk and testing each sample for lactose to see how long the capsules would last.

Maria Vitória worked with the university team for two full years until they landed on a prototype they loved. The capsules successfully took the lactose out of the milk and could be used for an entire *week*. That was much better than the pills that people had to take after eating a *single* dairy product! The reusable capsules were affordable *and* effective. Maria Vitória was thrilled that people with lactose intolerance would be able to enjoy milk products again without the burden of high costs.

Maria Vitória: "I decided to save the world. It's so cliché, but this is what I wanted. I wanted to save the world, transform lives, change realities, and make the world a better place."

And now, long after setting her goal, Maria Vitória could finally take her invention and findings to science fairs. And her teacher had been right—she won several local and regional awards that qualified her for the global fairs, including the Google Science Fair!

But to realize her dream, Maria Vitória had to make it through multiple rounds of submissions. She wrote up a report, making sure she explained her project clearly. She prepared milk samples. She practiced and recorded her presentation. And she sent it all to the judges. In a few weeks, they named her a regional finalist! But Maria Vitória still had to go through an intense interview process to make it to the international event. After multiple rounds, answering every question they flung at her, all she could do was wait to see if she would advance.

The day of the announcement finally arrived. Maria Vitória paced as she awaited the news. But when it came in, it was in English, so she had to wait even longer for the Portuguese translation. Finally, the news came through in a language Maria Vitória understood—she was officially named one of the global finalists! Maria Vitória's dream was coming true! She traveled to California to present her invention and became the first Latin American at the Google Science Fair.

The experience was everything she imagined it would be. Meeting fellow young inventors, touring the Google campus, and participating in award events felt so exciting. Even though Maria Vitória didn't win a prize, she felt proud of herself. And she still had another chance to place at a global fair.

Maria Vitória headed to the prestigious International Science and Engineering Fair (ISEF). She had another incredible experience. Just attending the biggest fair in the world felt like a huge honor. But again, she didn't even place among the top contenders. And this time, the disappointment hit hard.

Maria Vitória felt like her project was good enough to take home a prize. But reflecting on the fairs, she realized something was missing. Since she didn't speak English, a translator had to relay everything she said to the judges. The translators seemed to do a great job, but they didn't have the personal investment that Maria Vitória had for her invention. They hadn't spent years poring over the work or discovering solutions. So their direct translations fell a little flat. Maria Vitória wanted to learn English and come back with a new project that she could present on her own.

At sixteen years old, Maria Vitória returned home and jumped back into her research. But this time, she spent just as much time studying English. Formal classes were too expensive. Instead, she turned to YouTube videos, movies, and music to learn the language. After a year of hard work, she went back to ISEF ready to present her findings on bacterial infections.

But when her turn came, Maria Vitória got cold feet. She wasn't confident enough in her English and asked for another translator. This year, she understood enough to know for sure that the translations weren't capturing the true essence of her work and passion. She left the fair more determined than ever to return and speak for herself.

After another long year, Maria Vitória returned to the international fair for a third time, finally comfortable with her English. Able to speak freely, she delivered her presentation confidently. She shared her project with an enthusiasm that the translators had never been able to convey. And it paid off. She won third prize at the biggest science fair in the world and became the first girl to ever compete at ISEF three years in a row.

MARIA VITÓRIA WENT ON TO:

- Speak on the TEDx stage
- Find a more affordable treatment for yeast infections
- Win more than thirty national and international science fair awards

BISHOP CURRY V
OASIS CAR SEAT COOLER

10 Years Old
Texas, United States
2016

Bishop Curry V had always been a tinkerer. The homemade catapult in his garage (among other inventions) proved it. But one especially hot summer day, he found a challenge that would really put his abilities as an inventor to the test. Bishop was listening to the news with his family when a tragic story aired. A baby from their neighborhood had passed away after being left in a hot car.

This was the third time he had heard such sad news, and now it felt even more devastating . . . Bishop's little sister was the same age as the baby who had died. Bishop never wanted that to happen to her, or anyone else, and was determined to stop these terrible accidents.

Dropping everything, he sketched out his first idea in that very moment. He wanted to create a new "smart" car seat that could recognize when a baby was left in the car and call a grown-up to come back.

Bishop's father worked at Toyota, and Bishop hoped that the car company could help him develop a prototype of his idea. He asked his dad to talk to someone at work. But his parents didn't realize how dedicated Bishop was to his invention and didn't share his idea at first. They thought he would forget about it and get interested in something else. After all, most kids his age cared more about video

games or playing with friends than about car seat safety. But Bishop kept pestering them about it for two straight weeks. Finally, they saw his commitment and his dad took the idea to work.

Toyota was impressed. In fact, they were so impressed that they sent Bishop to a car seat safety convention. Bishop's original sketch had included all the bells and whistles a car seat could have—even a snack tray and music player. But at the event, he learned his invention didn't need any extras. It just needed to keep babies safe.

So Bishop wrote down the absolute essentials of his device. His final list was simple: recognize when a baby was left in the car, keep the baby cool, call the baby's caregiver, and if necessary, alert first responders. Bishop realized that it didn't even need to be a full car seat. Instead, it could simply attach to an already existing one.

Bishop gathered all the parts he thought he would need—a weight sensor, a thermometer, a fan, a GPS system, and a phone antenna. At first, Bishop tried to put all the parts on a wood board. But with everything spread out like that, it was way too big. It hardly fit in the car!

Bishop: "Don't let age limit your possibilities . . . Don't let limited resources limit your dreams . . . Let helping be your highest priority."

Another prototype tried to pack it all into a plastic cube that Bishop 3D-printed using a combination of Styrofoam and acetone. But the plastic melted in the heat! He finally found a good plastic to use and fit everything into the small box. But Bishop still had trouble getting all the parts to work right.

For his device to do everything he wanted, it needed to run like a computer. Bishop would have to learn to code. But there were so many kinds of code! Which one would be best for the car seat safety device? Bishop asked an engineer who recommended C++ because it would be easier to make changes. He couldn't take any fancy classes, so Bishop watched YouTube videos and taught himself the coding language.

Once he had a handle on the coding, Bishop used a circuit board to program the different elements of his car seat safety device. The weight sensor would tell the device when a baby was in the car seat. The GPS would show when the car stopped. The thermometer would keep track of the temperature and the fan would turn on if it got too hot. Then finally, the device would send a text message to a caregiver if the baby was left in the car. If the driver didn't come back and get the baby right away, the invention would call 911. Once all the coding was finished, Bishop needed to work on the physical product, and make sure each piece *actually* did what he coded it to do.

But early tests showed some problems. Like when Bishop's mom tossed her bag into the back seat and the weight sensors thought a baby was there. Bishop didn't want 911 responders coming to save a purse! So he changed out the weight sensor for a CO_2 sensor that could recognize a child's breathing. But that was way too expensive, so he traded it for a LiDAR sensor that could detect small movements

CONNECTING THE PIECES

A circuit board connects different electronic parts in a small space and lets them share information with each other. When a battery connects to a circuit board, the electricity runs through the circuit to the other pieces of the device in the order that you program.

AT THE SPEED OF LIGHT

LiDAR stands for "light detection and ranging" and uses light to measure distance. Light waves bounce off objects and back to the sensor. The sensor calculates distance based on how much time it takes the light waves to return.

like a chest rising and falling with each breath. And it worked! After seven failed prototypes, Bishop finally created a working model. He named his invention Oasis—a reminder of a sign of relief after scorching heat.

But the parts alone had cost more than $200! Bishop wanted every family to have access to his device. He needed to find a way to cut the costs without cutting quality. He hoped to hire an engineering firm to help. But that would cost money that he didn't have.

Bishop appeared on a local news show where a news anchor suggested a fundraising campaign to raise the money he needed to improve the design and even get a patent. Bishop thought it was a great idea. His family launched the campaign and donations came flooding in. Families who had lost children in hot car accidents, neighbors who loved the idea, and even complete strangers donated to his cause. After raising enough money, Bishop could hire the engineers he needed to help make final improvements to Oasis.

Over the next semester, Bishop worked with the engineers to tweak his invention. Luckily, his school was really supportive. They let him call the engineers during his lunch breaks to talk about the project. Bishop even used some of the money from his fundraising to fly from Texas to Georgia to work with them in person. With their help, Bishop swapped out some of the parts for more affordable pieces and made even more adjustments to Oasis. He eventually landed on a new model that attached to the headrest of the seat in front of a baby.

Now Bishop needed to run final tests to prove his invention worked. On hot summer days, he put a thermometer in a car and recorded his device's ability to keep the temperatures down. Based on the data, he adjusted the fan inside the Oasis to make sure it cooled the car enough to be safe. Bishop himself even sat in the car for twenty minutes at a time to make sure Oasis kept him cool. And it did! After a lot of hard work, he had finished the invention. Bishop knew that the Oasis would help keep his sister and other babies safe—and that was a wonderful feeling.

BISHOP WENT ON TO:

- Use the rest of the fundraising money to get a patent for Oasis
- Appear in a "Toyota Driver's Seat" video to talk about his device
- Appear on the TEDx stage
- Receive a letter from former president Bill Clinton, encouraging his work and thanking him for his invention

CASSIDY CROWLEY
BABY TOON

7 Years Old
Hawaii, United States
2016

Cassidy Crowley was a thoughtful big sister. She noticed that her baby sister loved chewing on her spoon after meals. But their mom worried that the baby would stick it too far down her throat and scratch herself, or maybe even choke. So when Cassidy had a chance to create an invention for a school project, she knew what she wanted to do. She set out to design a brand-new spoon that couldn't reach the back of a baby's throat.

First, Cassidy needed to do some background research to find out why her sister was chewing on the spoon in the first place. She learned that gnawing on things could soothe a baby's aching gums as their teeth grew in. Maybe the spoon could also work as a teether! Then Cassidy looked at existing baby spoons and forks to make sure nothing like what she envisioned had already been invented. Finally, she interviewed occupational therapists to learn how babies hold on to their utensils—with a full fist.

Next, Cassidy made a list of goals for her invention. It needed to be big enough that a baby couldn't fit it far into their mouth. It needed rounded corners without sharp, long points. It couldn't have

any small pieces or other choking hazards. It needed to be easy to hold with a full-fisted grasp. And it needed to be soft.

Cassidy's first prototype used a regular plastic fork with a squishy toy attached to the handle's tip. She made sure the toy was big enough so that babies couldn't get the long end of the fork into their mouths. But the toy came off easily and created a choking hazard. That was worse than the original!

For the next prototype, Cassidy decided to make it all one piece so it couldn't come apart. She used moldable plastic to create different shapes. Her favorites were animal shapes, but she struggled to get the plastic thin enough. Working with moldable plastic for the first time was hard!

Cassidy noted that future prototypes needed to be thinner, but she was on a roll and didn't want to lose her momentum. So she continued to tinker with the basic design. She could figure out how to make it thinner later. To add some style, Cassidy painted the entire thing with nail polish. She loved the look of the spoon with extra color, but obviously the nail polish

"Nontoxic" means that something won't hurt you if you eat it.

PROTECTING THE LOOK

Cassidy did not need a full utility patent. Instead, she applied for a design patent to protect her new creation. Remember, design patents protect a new design of an existing idea. Baby spoons already existed, but no one had created an elephant-shaped spoon/teether combination.

wasn't safe to eat from. She had a prototype, but not a *functional* prototype.

Cassidy tried again. This time, she understood the moldable plastic better and was able to craft a thinner, easy-to-hold elephant design. She also colored the plastic with a safe, nontoxic dye. This prototype was all one piece, big enough that it couldn't fit far back in a baby's mouth, and free from any sharp edges. Cassidy had met all her goals. The Baby Toon, named for its mix between a spoon and teether, was born.

Cassidy's teachers loved her project and encouraged her to make it more commercial so she could help even more babies. Her design was good, but using moldable plastic wasn't realistic for mass production. With help and support from her family, Cassidy partnered with a local company—3D Innovations—to improve the Baby Toon. First, Cassidy needed to find a new material for the spoon. She eventually chose silicone for its strength and flexibility. But it wasn't that easy. The first prototypes were too hard and would hurt a baby's teeth. They tried seven different types of silicone until they landed on the right softness for the Baby Toon. Firm enough to grasp, but soft enough to soothe a baby's growing teeth.

Cassidy was surprised at how long this process took—three

years had passed since she invented her first prototype of the Baby Toon.

But she couldn't stop now. With a design patent in hand and a final prototype ready, she partnered with a manufacturer, visited their factory, and learned all about the production process.

Cassidy's Baby Toon was finally ready to help families everywhere. Now parents wouldn't have to worry about their babies choking on spoons.

CASSIDY WENT ON TO:

- Receive a Certificate of Special Congressional Recognition for her work on the Baby Toon
- Be named the Student Entrepreneur of the Year by the Hawaii Venture Capital Association
- Teach other kids about inventing and entrepreneurship
- Appear on *Shark Tank* and receive a $50,000 investment
- Make a deal with Munchkin, one of the leading baby product brands in the United States, and sell the Baby Toon in more than four thousand stores across the nation

Cassidy: "Almost anyone can come up with a creative idea. But it takes a true entrepreneur to follow through and just keep on going, even when you have some hard times."

DASIA TAYLOR
COLOR-CHANGING STITCHES

16 Years Old
Iowa, United States
2020

Dasia Taylor had a passion for equity and inclusion. When her elementary school didn't have any plans to celebrate Black History Month, Dasia designed a bulletin board showcasing important African American trailblazers. When she got to junior high school and realized that the history lessons were slightly biased, she joined the Black History Game Show club to study the past from a more inclusive perspective. And when she was discouraged from participating in white-dominated spaces during high school, she co-chaired an equity advisory committee to make sure that everyone had the chance to do anything they wanted.

So when Dasia had the opportunity to invent something new, it made sense for her to look at it from an equity perspective. On the first day of her advanced chemistry class, Dasia's teacher invited the students to complete a personal science fair project on top of the regular classwork. Not everyone was interested, but Dasia signed up right away.

That day after school, Dasia went straight back to the chemistry lab and talked to her teacher about potential projects. She returned every day that week to read up on scientific advancements, looking for one that she could make more equitable.

One day, Dasia read about new infection-detecting stitches. The inventors hoped to use them in developing countries where regular stitches become infected in 10–30 percent of people who get them. Left undetected, the infections can lead to serious sickness, or even death. So the new stitches *seemed* like a good idea—able to detect the infections early—but they were really expensive to make, so only the wealthy would be able to use them. Plus, they relied on smartphone use, sending a notification to a device if they found infection. Dasia read that in developing countries, only about half the population owns a cell phone. And almost 75 percent of those who do own phones have older models, not smart devices. She realized that the people who needed the stitches most wouldn't even have access to them. Definitely not equitable.

Dasia decided that *she* would invent a better, more affordable version of infection-detecting stiches. If only she knew where to start. Before taking this chemistry class, she had never even been inside a lab. But she didn't let that stop her. She simply turned to mentors to help guide her, especially her own teacher.

First, Dasia had to learn about infections. Her teacher taught her that a person's skin is naturally acidic, with a pH level around 5. When infection sets in, the acidity goes down and the pH level rises to 9 or more, before any other signs of infection show up. Dasia needed to find a way to catch that change in pH early on. Her teacher told her about something called natural indicators—things like red cabbage, cherries, and beets that naturally change color when

Dasia: "I've done a lot of racial equity work in my community . . . So when I was presented with this opportunity to do research, I couldn't help but go at it with an equity lens."

THE PH SCALE

pH measures how acidic or basic something is and ranges from 0 to 14, with 7 being neutral. The lower the number, the more acidic. The higher the number, the more basic. Battery acid is the most acidic with a pH of 0, water is neutral with a pH of 7, and drain cleaner is the most basic with a pH of 14.

the pH level changes. Maybe she could develop color-changing stitches to find infection.

The hard thing would be to find a natural indicator that changed colors at the *right time*. Some of the indicators would change colors too soon—when the skin was still healthy. Purple cabbage juice, for example, stayed purple when added to a neutral pH solution of 7, but turned pink with a pH around 5, and turned teal with a higher pH of 9. It would be confusing to have the color change in both healthy and infected skin.

Dasia continued to research and test different natural indicators until she landed on beets. Beet juice stayed red until the pH level approached 9, the exact point to show infection! Now that she had her indicator, Dasia needed to figure out how to use it in stitches.

But just as she started working, the global COVID-19 pandemic closed her school. That might have made other students give up on their projects, but Dasia had equity work to do. She wasn't about to abandon it. And, luckily, some really great things came from that time. Since everyone was learning from home, the chemistry lab was empty all day. Dasia's principal agreed to let her into the building to keep working on the stitches. And since she was the only one in the school, it was easy to stay socially distanced and safe while spending four to five hours a day in the lab.

Still, Dasia had a lot to learn. She started by creating a solution of beet juice to color her stitches. She had to chop and boil dozens of beets to make the natural dye. Not realizing that she shouldn't pour ice-cold water into a beaker full of boiling-hot liquid, Dasia did just that—and the glass *shattered*, splattering her with bright red beet juice. Her clothes were ruined, but she learned never to do that again.

After a few months, Dasia landed on a good solution for her beet dye, but she had a hard time getting it to absorb into the thread. Traditional suture thread is nonabsorbent so that bacteria can't get into it, but that means it also wouldn't take up the beet color. Dasia had to find another option that would absorb the red solution while still being safe to use. She tried ten different materials until she found one that was strong enough to sew wounds together, the same thickness as traditional stitches, and able to hold on to the beet dye.

Now Dasia needed to test if her solution would still show infection once it was added to the thread. She stitched the red thread into a suture pad—a training cushion that students use to practice stitching before working on human patients. She treated each section with different pH solutions from 5 to 9. Only once the level reached a pH of 9 did the color change to a deep purple. Everything below stayed bright red. It was exactly what Dasia needed! She repeated the test many times to verify her findings and make sure that her color changing stitches truly did what she said they would do—show infection within five minutes of it setting in.

Dasia had created affordable and successful infection-detecting stitches. She participated in (and often won) many science fairs—spreading the word about her equitable invention. But at each event, she realized that she was the only Black inventor presenting. So she took the opportunity to not only promote her stitches, but also to call on science, technology, engineering, and mathematics (STEM) programs to do better with their diversity, equity, and inclusion initiatives.

Dasia knew that her success would help girls like her know they could accomplish absolutely anything they set their minds to. And because of her work, her old elementary school (which had continued her tradition of creating a bulletin board dedicated to celebrating Black History Month), showcased Dasia on their 2021 display—true history in the making.

DASIA WENT ON TO:

- Be named a finalist in the 2021 Regeneron Science Talent Search
- Appear in the news and on television
- Continue her research at the University of Iowa
- Teach other students about invention and research techniques

PROTOTYPES

> It's kind of difficult in the beginning but just keep trying because you'll eventually get it.
>
> —Shakeena Julio, thirteen-year-old inventor of the energy scooter

We've talked a lot about prototypes in this book. So you have probably already figured out that a prototype is a model or test design of a new idea or invention. But there are actually lots of different kinds of prototypes, so let's look closely at a few.

Diagrams or **sketches** get early ideas down on paper without building a physical model. This type of prototype is useful to look back on and help you develop plans moving forward. A drawing will guide you to know what materials you need, where things will fit together, and what each part will (hopefully) do.

Digital prototypes use computer-assisted design (CAD) or other programs to create a digital model of an invention. These are more precise than hand-drawn sketches because you can input exact dimensions, shapes, sizes, and more.

Physical models don't have working parts but are meant to give an overall idea of the design. You might use building blocks, toys, or craft supplies to put together this kind of prototype. It won't work properly, but it will give you a place to start, help you look at things on a smaller scale before creating the full invention, and give you a good idea of what needs to come next.

Proof-of-principle prototypes are quick models to test if an idea will work. They might not have all the same pieces that later prototypes will have, and usually aren't made with the same materials. But they'll show you if something will work before you get into more technical designs.

Functional prototypes test both function and design but might not be the same size or use the same materials as a final product. These prototypes make sure an invention is going to work the way you want it to.

Working prototypes closely mirror the final product. These prototypes try to use the same materials, the same size, and the same parts that your final product will use.

SO WHAT KIND OF PROTOTYPE WILL YOU NEED?

Well . . . you might need all of them. Or at least quite a few. Inventing is a process. The key is to test each prototype, see what works and what doesn't, and then make another, better version of your invention. You might go through just a handful of prototypes, or you might need 20, 30, or even more. But none of them are wasted. Even if something feels like a failure, remember that you can learn from *every* model. And each one gets you another step closer to a finished, working invention.

INVENTIONS IN TECHNOLOGY

When you learn to code, you give yourself a tool, a tech superpower, to create change in your community. You use your voice, your mind, and your skills to find solutions to problems.

–Reshma Saujani, founder of *Girls Who Code*

STEVE WOZNIAK
ADDER/SUBTRACTOR

Steve Wozniak didn't just *understand* math and electronics. He was a wiz. By the time he was eight years old, he had mastered things that many adults couldn't figure out. He understood how electrons moved to create electricity. He knew how diodes, transistors, and resistors worked. And even from that early age, he wanted to use his brain to do something good for the world.

Steve grew up in Sunnyvale, California. Back then, the area was on the verge of a technological revolution that later earned it the name Silicon Valley. Steve's dad worked for the new electronic and engineering companies in the area, so Steve got to use the cool parts his dad brought home from work.

Steve constantly tinkered with the electronics and always wanted to do more with them. So in fifth grade, when he stumbled across a science magazine about computers, he was hooked on the idea.

Back then, this was new and super-exciting technology. But computers of that time weren't the laptops and desktops of today. The ENIAC, the computer that Steve had read about, cost $400,000 to make—equal to more than $3.5 million today! And it was HUGE! It filled an entire room, used more than six thousand switches, and weighed about thirty tons. It obviously wasn't something people could keep in their living rooms. But Steve dreamed of inventing a computer for the masses—something that everyday people could afford and use at home.

Steve had created many first-place science fair projects before, but he decided that his sixth-grade entry would be different. That year, he would work on a *computerized* project. He studied his magazines and learned from his dad. Soon he grasped the math and language used in computers. Binary numbers made up of 1s and 0s (which stood for "on" or "off"), used logic to tell the computer how to do different tasks.

Steve used all that understanding to create an electronic version of tic-tac-toe using logic gates—electronic components that control electricity. He spent many long weeks programming the game by playing every possible version. And it worked! He knew he could win the science fair with his new invention . . . until smoke began spewing from the device only days before the event.

Steve: "The world needs inventors—great ones. You can be one. If you love what you do and are willing to do what it takes, it's within your reach. And it'll be worth every minute you spend."

Steve had no idea what had gone wrong. And he didn't have time to figure it out and fix it before the fair. But despite that disappointment, he knew he was one step closer to his dream of inventing a personal computer.

His tic-tac-toe game had been fun, but Steve didn't think it was all that useful. In eighth grade, he set a goal to build a basic computer that could do something more worthwhile—add and subtract.

Steve started with the basic principles of logic gates that he had learned from his tic-tac-toe game. But now things were about to get even more complicated when he connected those gates to switches representing binary numbers to be added or subtracted. When the switches turned on, electricity would flow through to a line of lights, representing the sum (again, in binary numbers).

Steve created two rows of ten switches each. If the switches were off, they stood for zeros. If the switches were on, they represented ones. For example, if Steve wanted to show the number 3 in the top row (0000000011 in binary), he turned on the two switches to the farthest right—eight switches off, and two on. If he wanted to show the number 4 in the bottom row (0000000100 in binary), he turned on the switch third from the right (and kept all the others off). Steve then plugged connectors into holes across a plastic board and soldered transistors, resistors, and diodes together, creating his series of logic gates.

When adding, the invention would start on the rightmost column and send electricity based on which switches were on and which were off. If only one switch in a column was turned on, the light in that column also came on. If neither switch was on in a column, the light below did not turn on either.

3	0000000011	□□□□□□□□■■	SWITCH ROW 1
+4	+0000000100	□□□□□□□■□□	SWITCH ROW 2
7	0000000111	○○○○○○○●●●	LIGHTS

Things got tricky when both switches were on in one column. When that happened, the light stayed off because the electricity

Binary numbers are written with only 0s and 1s. For example:

Decimal	Binary
0	0000000000
1	0000000001
2	0000000010
3	0000000011
4	0000000100
5	0000000101
6	0000000110
7	0000000111
8	0000001000
9	0000001001
10	0000001010

In a computer, 1 represents "on" and 0 represents "off."

ELECTRICITY IN MOTION

Logic gates are the building blocks of electronics. They have one or more input (where electricity flows in) and only one output (where electricity can potentially flow out). They either send electricity through or stop it from going farther.

There are many types of logic gates. Let's take a look at the three that Steve would have needed. Remember, 1 stands for "on" and 0 stands for "off."

AND gates output a 1 only if both inputs are 1.

Input A	Input B	Output
1	1	1
1	0	0
0	1	0
0	0	0

OR gates output a 1 if one or both inputs are 1.

Input A	Input B	Output
1	1	1
1	0	1
0	1	1
0	0	0

OR gates output a 1 if *only* one but *not* both inputs are 1.

Input A	Input B	Output
1	1	0
1	0	1
0	1	1
0	0	0

carried into the next column to the left. Steve had to show true electronics know-how to make that happen. And once the current carried over, there was even more to do. If there were no switches on in the new column, then the light there would turn on.

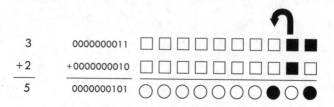

If one switch was on in the new column, then the light stayed off and the electricity carried once again to a third column. If *both* switches were already on in the new column, then the light both turned on *and* passed electricity along to a third column.

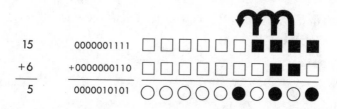

The process continued across all ten columns until the answer displayed in lights. If a light turned on, it represented a one. If it stayed off, it represented a zero. So, if the three right-most lights came on, it represented 0000000111, binary for seven.

Steve had learned from his earlier mistake with the tic-tac-toe board, so he used plenty of resistors to keep this invention from getting too hot. But, when he tested it, the electricity wasn't always going the direction it needed to. Fortunately, when Steve looked at it closely, he saw the problem right away. Some of those extra resistors were letting the current go through to the wrong place. So Steve changed some of the resistors to diodes to get the electrons to flow properly.

The project ultimately used more than 100 transistors, 200 resistors, and 200 diodes, plus all the switches, wires, and lights. Steve's computer could add or subtract any number up to 1,023—the highest he could reach with his board (because in binary numbers, 1,023 is written as 1111111111—the number displayed when all ten lights were on).

After months of working on the project, Steve's calculator finally worked seamlessly. Each time he put in a problem, the answer showed up in the lights on the electronic display. Steve Wozniak had built a basic computer. And unlike the room-filling ENIAC, it was small enough to carry! He named it the Adder/Subtractor and prepared to present at the science fair.

Unfortunately, when Steve got to the event, the awards had already been given out—before any of the students had a chance to talk about their projects. And Steve was only given an honorable mention. He and the other participants were confused. They all knew that the Adder/Subtractor was beyond impressive. So it didn't take long for Steve to realize that the judging was biased. The winners were all members of the group hosting the event.

Steve didn't let that stop him from sharing his invention. And soon after, the United States Air Force made sure that Steve got the recognition he deserved. They awarded him their top prize for an electronics project. He beat out high school seniors when he was only in eighth grade.

The Adder-Subtractor gave Steve so much confidence that he began to believe he could do absolutely anything with electronics. This first breakthrough was one of many on Steve's path to bring at-home computers to the masses.

STEVE WENT ON TO:

- Co-found Apple Computers
- Invent the Apple I and Apple II, the first successful home computers
- Be inducted into The National Inventor's Hall of Fame
- Appear in multiple interviews and documentaries
- Write his memoir, *iWoz: Computer Geek to Cult Icon: How I Invented the Personal Computer, Co-Founded Apple, and Had Fun Doing It*

KELVIN DOE
HOMEMADE BATTERY AND GENERATOR

13 Years Old
Sierra Leone, Africa
2008

Day after day, Kelvin Doe sat in a dark house because the power in his neighborhood was beyond unreliable—it only turned on about once a week! This made lots of things impossible. The worst part was that without electricity, he couldn't listen to his favorite songs. And music was huge to Kelvin. He loved enjoying and sharing his favorite tunes, and even dreamed of being a DJ someday. But that wouldn't be possible without more consistent power.

Kelvin wasn't the only one fed up with the darkness. His neighbors felt frustrated too. Kelvin wanted to bring power to his home *and* community. But at the time, he had no idea how to do it.

Luckily, Kelvin's love of music also led him to a deep interest in electronics and engineering. He wanted to know how things like radios, CD players, and DVD players worked. But he didn't have access to classes, or money to buy the newest technologies. Still, he didn't let those limitations stop him. Kelvin visited the local dump and searched for old, tossed-out electronics, determined to teach himself how they worked.

Every night, Kelvin went to bed especially early. He slept for about five hours and woke up when he was sure the rest of his family

was asleep. He needed the space and the quiet to focus as he took apart the electronics from the dump and studied how the pieces fit together. Often, his mom would wake up in the middle of the night to find the living room floor covered with wires. Now their *house* looked like a dump! Worried about Kelvin's health, his mom insisted he get more sleep.

Kelvin: "Creativity is universal and can be found in places where one does not expect to find it. And perseverance and passion are essential to nurturing that creative ability."

Kelvin wanted to listen to his mom, but he *couldn't* stop working. He tried to catch a bit more sleep, but still snuck awake extra early to study and work. Each new gadget showed him more about electronics.

Kelvin learned so much that he could eventually fix his neighbors' broken radios. He even built his own new gadgets by salvaging working parts from the trash he found in the dump. Kelvin's favorite creations were an amplifier and mixer. By adding cardboard and scrap metal to the working electronics parts, he created an entire sound system to share music with his neighbors.

A sound amplifier makes sound quality better and clearer. A mixer combines sounds and can adjust the levels of each part, like bass and vocals.

Kelvin used his new tools to finally become a DJ. He named himself DJ Focus and played at parties in his neighborhood. People would pay him for his services, but he had to use most of the money to buy batteries to power his sound system for the next event. So Kelvin decided to *make* a battery. And once again, he would have to teach himself how to do it.

First, Kelvin needed to understand exactly how batteries worked. He took apart an old battery and studied its pieces. He saw different metals and some type of battery acid inside. He learned that electrons flow from a negative end to a positive end once connected to a wire. Then he found the parts he needed from the dump and got to work.

But building a battery was harder than Kelvin expected, and he spent many late nights frustrated by the project. Eventually he figured out how to supply both a positive and a negative charge. He had enough money from DJing to buy the battery acid, and once he added it, the electrons could flow. Kelvin wrapped the whole thing in tape and ran some tests. He connected the battery to a lightbulb and cheered! The bulb shone brightly! Kelvin had invented a homemade

A SMALL TUBE WITH MASSIVE POWER

Batteries work by converting chemical energy to electrical energy. A chemical reaction inside the battery makes the electrons want to move from the negative end to the positive end. (And remember, when electrons move, they create electricity.) But a substance inside the battery called an electrolyte stops the movement within the battery itself, otherwise the reaction would happen before a battery was put into place, and it would die before even being useful. Once a battery connects to an appliance or wire, it creates a path for the electrons to travel, powering the gadget on the way. Once the chemical reaction ends, electrons no longer flow, and the battery dies.

GENERATING EVEN MORE POWER

Electric generators convert mechanical energy into electricity by using magnetism. A power source like gasoline, water, or wind spins a coil between the poles of a horseshoe-shaped magnet. That coil cuts through the magnetic field, making an electrical current flow through the coil. The generator can then store the electricity in batteries or send it directly where needed.

battery. He wouldn't have to buy the expensive ones to share music at parties and other events anymore.

Neighbors took notice and realized that the invention could bring much needed power to their community. They asked Kelvin to make them their own batteries, and paid Kelvin enough to buy the acid. The rest of the materials he found at the dump. And soon, Kelvin and his neighbors all had power. For the first time ever, they could turn on their lights every day!

DJing at parties made Kelvin realize just how much he loved sharing his music. He wanted to create a radio station to take his songs and thoughts to the entire community. But his battery alone wasn't strong enough to power the station. So Kelvin decided to build a generator to create an even stronger current. He gathered more scraps from the dump, including a capacitor and spark plug to store, deliver, and regulate the electricity. He built the entire thing inside of a cardboard box and soon had all the power he needed!

Finally, Kelvin could expand his DJ dreams. He created an entire FM radio station, once again inventing each component with trash and discarded electronics. He had already brought change to his community as a self-taught inventor. Now Kelvin could shed light with his words as DJ Focus.

KELVIN WENT ON TO:

- Be a finalist in the first Innovate Salone contest, a high school invention challenge in his country
- Travel to the Massachusetts Institute of Technology as the youngest ever "visiting practitioner"
- Appear in a viral YouTube video that led to an invitation to speak on the TEDx stage
- Start the Kelvin Doe Foundation to help kids throughout Sierra Leone invent solutions to daily problems in their community

FATIMA AL KAABI
PHOTO-TAKING ROBOT

10 Years Old
Dubai,
United Arab Emirates
2009

Fatima Al Kaabi wanted to learn everything she could about robots. So much so that she would spend hours a day locked away in her room watching internet videos, studying articles, and poring over books, devouring everything she could find about robotics. Her parents—both engineers themselves—encouraged her passion. They bought Fatima beginner's kits and guided her in creating simple projects, but Fatima wanted more than toys. She wanted to make *real* robots.

One day, after watching a TED talk by a successful inventor, Fatima felt more inspired than ever. She hoped to make her own robots impressive enough to present on the TED stage. But when she asked for guidance, her teacher said a child could never reach that goal. She told Fatima to forget about her dream for at least ten years, and that even then it would be a long shot. But instead of being discouraged, Fatima set out to prove her teacher wrong!

Fatima searched for a mentor and tried to enroll in a coding program. But she soon learned that there were not many opportunities for young girls in her country to learn about science, technology, engineering, and mathematics (STEM). But she would not be dissuaded. If she couldn't find a teacher, she would figure things out on her own.

Fatima turned to internet videos and tutorials to learn all sorts of robotics skills.

By the time she was ten years old, Fatima was ready to create her first major invention—a robot that took instant pictures. Her friends loved using a Polaroid camera and seeing their images printed on film seconds after pushing a button. Fatima knew it would be even more fun if they could all be in the frame. And how cool would it be if a *robot* took the picture?

With a clear idea in mind, Fatima started building her robot. She crafted and built a metal base and arms. She added a sensor to measure the distance between the robot and the people in front of the camera. She programmed it to move back and forth to get everyone in the frame before the robotic arm pressed the camera button.

Fatima's first prototype looked great, and the robot itself did everything she had programmed it to do. Until Fatima tried taking her first picture. The camera didn't stay in place when she put it on the robot. Sometimes it shifted so much that the robotic arms couldn't reach the button at all. Other times, it moved just enough that the picture came out blurry. And sometimes it fell off completely.

Trying to fix the problem, Fatima redesigned the base of the robot. But even with a sturdier foundation, the camera *still* fell. Next, Fatima tried adding support beams, but they got in the way and stopped her from changing out the film. She even tried taping the camera down! After six failed prototypes and many rolls of wasted film, she crafted a holder with four corner pieces that held on tightly to the camera. She added elastic bands for extra support and ran another set of tests. Finally, the robot moved into position and pushed a button without the camera leaning or falling! The pictures came out clear every time.

Fatima displayed her invention at a national convention where it was a big hit! People loved interacting with the robot and were amazed at Fatima's achievement.

ENGINEERING + PROGRAMMING = ROBOTICS

Robotics uses a combination of engineering and computer programming. Building the physical robot requires mechanical engineering. Getting it to think and act on its own requires computer engineering. And making it run on electricity requires electrical engineering. Then the robot can be programmed to do a specific task. Properly designed, a robot should be able to make decisions and carry out a task automatically.

But back at school, Fatima still faced opposition. Even after proving her abilities in robotics, her teachers still wouldn't take her seriously. Some thought her projects were cute little crafts, while others refused to give her the same resources that they gave to the male students. Fatima refused to let that stop her and continued inventing. She transferred to two new schools, until she finally found a place where the teachers gave her a chance and supported her dreams. She improved her robotics skills and invented more complex projects.

Finally, Fatima's big break came from a youth center in her community when they nominated her for the thing she still wanted most—a chance to speak on the TEDx stage. Multiple interviews and a grueling wait later, Fatima finally got the news she had been waiting for: She'd been chosen to speak at the event held in her very own community! At fourteen years old, Fatima proved her teachers wrong and achieved her dream of presenting on the TEDx stage.

Fatima spoke about how ideas shouldn't be limited by age or gender. She shared the troubles she had with getting the support she needed as a young female inventor. She told the attendees

ROBOTS VS. MACHINES

The difference between a true robot and a machine is that a robot should function with minimal human interaction (humans send instructions through programming and the robot does the task alone), while a machine can accomplish the same task with full human assistance. In this example, the camera is a machine. It could print instant pictures if a person held it, got in position, and pushed the button. But Fatima's robot did all those things on its own after she programmed it correctly.

that she couldn't receive a patent in her own country because of gender discrimination. And she called on the government to make needed change.

People listened. Fatima was honored by the vice president of the United Arab Emirates (UAE) and named as the country's youngest inventor. Because of this recognition from the government, Fatima's efforts, and the work of fellow Emirati inventors, girls in the UAE now have access to the STEM education and patent opportunities that Fatima could only dream of.

FATIMA WENT ON TO:

- Create twelve more inventions by the time she was fifteen years old, including a solar bag that charged electronic devices, a belt to help the hearing impaired, and a robot that could attend school and record lessons for sick children while they were in the hospital
- Teach girls about STEM and the importance of inventing
- Appear multiple times on the TEDx stage
- Attend college to study artificial intelligence

ANN MAKOSINSKI
HOLLOW FLASHLIGHT

15 Years Old
British Columbia,
Canada
2012

Ann Makosinski didn't have a room full of dolls, blocks, or stuffed animals like other kids did. Her parents wanted to really push her creativity and imagination, so they encouraged Ann to make her *own* fun. When they did give her a "toy," it was something like a box of transistors. That's what happens when your parents are engineers.

Ann played with these gadgets while her parents worked on their own projects. Soon she had her first inventions, toys made of cardboard and glue. She talked for hours about what they each did, imagining an entirely new world. Though her first inventions never *actually* worked, she didn't care. She was creating. They were real to Ann.

This instilled in Ann the foundation for a life of science. When she was eleven years old, she entered the sixth-grade science fair and was immediately hooked. It was thrilling to share her findings with others. Her first project (comparing different laundry soaps) was interesting, but Ann wanted a project that she felt was ready to take to bigger fairs. From that time, she entered her local fair every year, determined to advance.

Then, the summer before ninth grade, Ann traveled to the Philippines to visit her family, and made a new friend on the trip. After

returning home, the girls stayed in contact, and a few months later Ann's friend shared that she wasn't currently in school—she had failed the year before. The friend's family didn't have electricity, and during the daylight hours, she had to help with chores around the house. That didn't leave much time for homework while the sun was up. And without light to study by in the evenings, she fell behind on her schoolwork.

Ann knew she could help and set out to create a light that didn't need a power supply. She studied flashlights that used pressure or resistance to generate electricity. Ann even made such a light using a gear and crank. It worked, but similar lights already existed. And she thought using the crank was tiring and loud. Plus, she had to use both hands to turn on the light—one to hold it still, and one to crank. It was hard to focus the light on something specific, like a page of homework.

By this time, Ann's friend had moved to a bigger city and finally had in-home electricity. But Ann still wanted to come up with a better flashlight, even if her friend didn't need it anymore. There must be other kids who could use her light. And if nothing else, she could take whatever she came up with to her next science fair.

Ann went back to the drawing board. As she researched natural sources of energy, she learned that the human body generates enough energy to power a hundred-watt lightbulb! Most of that is used to keep our bodies functioning, but a lot of it is wasted.

Ann: "Anything really is possible. Anything you pursue as long as you dream about it . . . You can reach your dreams. It is possible."

Ann thought back to a school assignment she had done many years before. Back in sixth grade, she had used a candle to warm Peltier tiles and create electricity. Ann hoped that body heat from her hand could do the same thing and power a flashlight filled with the tiles.

Peltier tiles are small squares that can turn heat into electricity when one side of the tile is heated while the other side is cooled.

But her experiments showed that Peltier tiles alone wouldn't provide enough energy to power three LED lightbulbs. So she built a circuit board to amplify the power.

But Ann knew that the tiles would only work with heat on one side and cool air on the other. If the hand holding her flashlight warmed both sides of the tiles, the light wouldn't turn on. So Ann mounted the tiles and circuit board onto an aluminum tube. Then she cut a section out of a PVC pipe and slid it over the aluminum. With the hole exposing the Peltier tiles, the heat from her hand warmed the top side while cool air passed through the hollow tube beneath. This time, the flashlight shone brightly the moment she grabbed it— just from her body heat!

Ann was thrilled that the light actually worked. She proudly named her invention the Hollow Flashlight, certain it was one of the best things she had ever made. Since she still loved science fairs, she submitted the project to the Google Science Fair

Peltier tiles work best with a bigger temperature difference between the warm and cool sides.

and was chosen as one of the top fifteen finalists! She presented to the judges and discussed her work with many school groups. People loved the flashlight that worked just by picking it up!

But to Ann, the other projects seemed levels above her own. At the end of the event, she worried that her flashlight wasn't good enough. So imagine her surprise when her name and picture appeared during the awards ceremony. After years of participating in science fairs, Ann finally won the top prize in her age group for the Hollow Flashlight.

ANN WENT ON TO:

- Appear on *The Tonight Show with Jimmy Fallon*
- Invent the eDrink, a mug that used extra heat from a hot drink to charge a cell phone
- Receive patents for both of her inventions
- Present at schools and science events
- Give multiple TEDx talks about her inventions
- Be named one of *Forbes* magazine's "30 Under 30" and *Popular Science* magazine's Young Inventor of the Year

SAMAIRA MEHTA
CODERBUNNYZ

Not many six-year-olds know how to code. And even fewer *love* to code. But Samaira Mehta was one of those rare few. And it all started with a prank. Her dad put her in front of a computer and told her to click a link that said, "Press this if you're beautiful." But when Samaira tried to click it, the link disappeared every time!

She was confused and wanted to know what was happening. Did her dad think she wasn't beautiful? Was there something wrong with the computer? Her dad told her not to worry—it was just a prank. Something he had created using *code*. Samaira had never heard of code before. She needed to know more.

Samaira's dad taught her that code was a language that computers could understand. He showed her that code uses many lines of step-by-step instructions (called an algorithm) to tell a computer what to do in different situations. Then he slowly taught her how to code. Samaira learned how to create the same prank that he had done and then moved on to bigger projects. Within a year, she had coded mazes, games, and even a calculator.

Samaira was hooked. She assumed that her friends would love her new passion too. But when she asked them about it, they thought coding was boring, hard, or frustrating.

Samaira couldn't believe her friends hated coding! She wanted to prove that it was fun. She knew her friends loved playing board games together, so Samaira figured they'd enjoy coding if they could learn it through a game.

Samaira drew her first ideas on scraps of paper and glued them onto pieces of cardboard to make a game board and pawns. She didn't love her kid-like drawings, though, so she tried some computer designs instead. But graphic design is not easy for a seven-year-old, and nothing was working out. So she went back to the hand-drawn versions. Samaira spent all summer working on her new game, CoderBunnyz, which used coding principles to help a bunny gather enough carrots, avoid obstacles, and reach its destination.

But CoderBunnyz was still just some hand-drawn ideas glued to a cut-up cardboard box. Samaira didn't want to share it with her friends when it looked like a little kid's craft project.

Still, the game had great potential as an introduction to coding. So she asked her parents to make her idea into a real-life board game. They were supportive, but they encouraged her to work out the problem on her own.

Samaira: "Learning is a lot easier when it's fun!"

Samaira researched and learned she needed clear sketches, a working prototype, and proven game testing. Then she would need to find a graphic designer and a production team to finalize her work. Samaira showed her parents all she had found. They were impressed and agreed to pay for the next steps.

Samaira and her parents visited a local shop many times to print

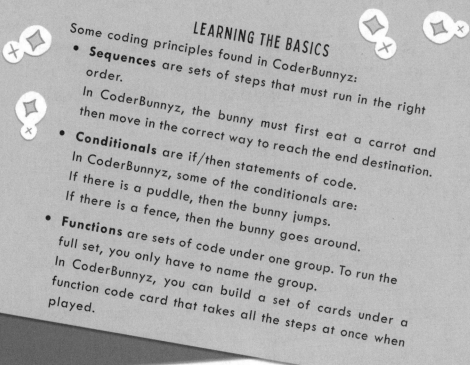

LEARNING THE BASICS

Some coding principles found in CoderBunnyz:

- **Sequences** are sets of steps that must run in the right order.
  In CoderBunnyz, the bunny must first eat a carrot and then move in the correct way to reach the end destination.
- **Conditionals** are if/then statements of code.
  In CoderBunnyz, some of the conditionals are:
  If there is a puddle, then the bunny jumps.
  If there is a fence, then the bunny goes around.
- **Functions** are sets of code under one group. To run the full set, you only have to name the group.
  In CoderBunnyz, you can build a set of cards under a function code card that takes all the steps at once when played.

each of Samaira's sketches on glossy paper. Now they started to look more official! After several tests and new drawings, Samaira knew she was ready to work with a graphic design team for a more professional touch. She sent her drawings and cardboard prototypes to the team and paid them to create expert sketches. She couldn't wait to see how they brought her designs to life.

Finally, the package arrived. Samaira tore it open, anxious to see the art. But when she pulled out the new images, her heart fell. They weren't at all what she had envisioned. And she didn't like what she saw. Although the design team was clearly talented, they had created a *realistic* bunny, carrots, and setting, while Samaira wanted the game to look more *computer*-like. After all, it was supposed to simulate coding. Samaira realized she hadn't communicated her vision to them clearly enough.

Samaira went back to the team and made sure they understood her ideas. They adjusted everything from the bunny design to the carrot colors to the placement of each image on the cards. After eight months of back-and-forth emails and modifications, CoderBunnyz was finished.

Her friends agreed to play the game and actually enjoyed it! They learned different coding principles like sequence, conditionals, and functions—all skills that could transfer to real-life computer programming. But they had some ideas for even more improvements. The game already featured a pool, movie theater, park, and carnival. Her friends suggested adding a school and a zoo to the bunny's route. Samaira took their recommendations and made the final tweaks to her game. The graphic design team made the changes, and Samaira produced five boxes of the game—enough to give to her friends and to use herself.

But playing with her friends made Samaira realize how much she loved teaching kids to code. She expanded her efforts, printed more games, and offered workshops to other kids using CoderBunnyz. And now no one complained that coding was boring or too hard. Samaira had made coding fun for kids of all ages.

SAMAIRA WENT ON TO:

- Mass produce CoderBunnyz for at-home use after many parent requests at her coding events
- Top the Amazon charts with a #1 bestseller
- Develop CoderMindz and CoderMarz to teach more about coding and artificial intelligence
- Launch two coding programs: Girls U Code and Yes, One Billion Kids Can Code
- Teach more than seven hundred coding workshops across the world to over 25,000 kids

RIYA KARUMANCHI
SMARTCANE

13 Years Old
Ontario, Canada
2017

Riya Karumanchi took the conveniences of her life for granted. Daily tasks were so much easier for her than they had ever been for her grandparents, or even her parents, because of big technological advancements, but she didn't yet realize it—until she took a family trip to India. There, Riya made a friend who had to drop out of school to work as a maid to help support her family. That friend didn't have things like computers or smartphones, or even in-home appliances, to make life easier. She had to do a lot of things by hand. And that took so much time that school wasn't an option anymore. It was the first time that Riya realized that the people around her might not have the same luxuries that she did.

Soon after, Riya met her friend's visually impaired grandma, and found yet another place where technology hadn't been shared equally. She watched her friend's grandma bump into tables and other things that were above waist level, even though she was using a white cane. The cane was helpful at ground level. But it didn't catch the higher obstacles.

Riya headed home to research the white cane. Though it had been around for almost 100 years, hardly any updates had been made.

Despite how far technology had moved forward in that time, the cane was little more than a simple stick.

Over the next semester, Riya talked to many visually impaired people to understand their thoughts on the white cane and listen to their needs. One person told her that the cane couldn't warn them if a side-view mirror from a car parked in the street was hanging over the sidewalk. Another talked about running into low-hanging branches. And all of them shared their hopes for something better. So Riya decided to use the technology she loved to create an updated cane for the visually impaired that could navigate around *all* obstacles.

Riya knew it was important to work closely with the visually impaired community on the invention. They understood the limitations of the white cane and were the only ones to really recognize the needed updates. They proved invaluable in the process and helped her understand their saying, "Nothing for us, without us." Riya took that message to heart and consistently partnered with the visually impaired community in her efforts.

Her first idea was to make a pair of "smart shoes" that vibrated to warn the wearers of potential obstacles and give directions using GPS navigation. But Riya soon realized the shoes would have even more drawbacks than the white cane. If they lost power, for example, a person would be left completely stranded. The blind community told Riya that the white cane was familiar and useful. So why not simply update it to include more advanced technology?

Riya: "The future is just a vision, until we all work together to create it . . . Let's start building the future that we want to live in today."

Riya brainstormed ideas and wrote up a report with her solutions. She took her theories to a few science fairs and even won multiple awards for the ideas. But that's all she had: ideas. Riya wanted to make a real difference but didn't have the skills it would take to make a working prototype on her own. So she went to a Hackathon—an event where people formed teams to develop new technology extremely quickly. The event would be taxing—Riya would only have two days of intense work to complete the project. But with a clear plan, she knew she could do it with the right people on board.

Even though Riya was only thirteen years old when she presented her idea at the event, she soon had eight adults committed to her project. Together, they pushed through a little stress and ran on even littler sleep until they were able to finish a working prototype of the SmartCane within the time limit.

The new device used an ultrasonic sensor to recognize obstacles at all levels and warn the user of any approaching hurdles. But Riya

WHERE IN THE WORLD?

GPS stands for Global Positioning System. It shows people exactly where they are on the globe within only a few yards. GPS works through a system of 31 satellites that each circle the globe twice a day. Receivers (like the ones found in smartphones and cars) are always listening for signals from the satellites. Once they connect to at least four, they can gauge exactly where they are in the world. Receivers then use the same method to figure out the distance to a destination and give directions to the new location. The United States created and maintains the GPS system, while Russia invented a similar system called GLONASS. Together, the two programs make up the global navigation satellite system.

SOUND MEASURES DISTANCE

Ultrasonic sensors send out sound waves to measure the distance between the sensor and surrounding objects. They calculate the distance based on the time it takes for the sound wave to come back after bouncing off an object.

and her team didn't stop there. They added GPS tracking and navigation. The SmartCane gave directions by vibrating once for "turn left" and twice for "turn right." The team presented the prototype at the end of the Hackathon and won the People's Choice Award for the invention. And even better—Riya landed an internship at a local college to learn more about the technologies used in the SmartCane.

Riya woke up at 6:30 a.m. every day that summer to catch a bus to her internship. But it was worth it. She learned so much. By the end of the summer, she had even more ideas to improve her invention. So she attended another Hackathon, called HackABILITY, which focused on technologies specifically for accessibility. And this time, Riya's team included a member of the visually impaired community. Working together, they fixed some bugs in the previous prototype and added computer vision to the SmartCane. Now it could describe a person's surroundings and even recognize faces to tell the user when someone was approaching.

The HackABILITY event was a huge success. And this time, SmartCane and Riya's team won! Now that she had a prototype that she felt certain about, Riya wanted to take the cane to market so it could help the entire visually impaired community. Before, Riya had struggled to get financial donations and technical support. No one would take a young girl seriously. Many had sent her away without

COMPUTER VISION

Computer vision is a type of artificial intelligence (AI) that lets computers gather and use information from images. It tries to replicate the human eye.

even listening. But with the HackABILITY win, Riya finally found people who were interested in providing the financial help she needed. She got her first backer and soon more donations came in. By the time she was fifteen years old, Riya became the CEO of her own company and worked to take SmartCane to market.

RIYA WENT ON TO:

- Give TEDx and Women in IT speeches to advocate for equality in technological advancement
- Teach others about AI and computer vision
- Be named one of the Top 20 Teen Entrepreneurs and Innovators in the world by TeenBusiness Media

YUMA SOERIANTO
"LET'S STACK AR!" IPHONE APP

10 Years Old
Melbourne, Australia
2017

School was a breeze for six-year-old Yuma Soerianto. He finished quickly and got bored easily. He tried filling his extra time by watching TV, but the shows didn't interest him either. In his search for something challenging but fun, he started learning about technology. He wanted to learn how computers worked, how websites ran, and how virtual games played seamlessly. It all seemed like magic.

There weren't many classes in his area about computer technology, so Yuma turned to the internet. He watched videos about programming and quickly learned the basics of computer code. Yuma was a natural! He started a personal website, coded virtual greeting cards, and developed online computer games. His friends liked his games, but they were even *more* interested in cell phone games and apps.

Yuma loved the idea of another challenge and turned his focus to app development. It was completely different from the web design he had learned. And much harder. Yuma learned about Swift—a new programming language developed by Apple to create apps that worked on their devices. He watched all the tutorials he could find on the internet, but he still didn't feel ready to create a full app.

Yuma asked his teachers for help. But he soon realized that he

knew as much about coding as they did. Maybe more! And there still weren't any coding classes in his town that would accept a kid. So he turned to the internet once again. Yuma found a free online Swift coding course offered by Stanford University and enrolled in the class. Taking a college-level class as an eight-year-old wasn't easy. He often had to pause a lesson to study things like trigonometry (advanced math that older students would have already known). But he refused to give up and, in only four months, he finished the course, confident in his coding abilities.

Now it was time to put his knowledge to use. Yuma brainstormed ideas for new apps, sketched prototypes in a notebook, and did all the coding. But he also wanted his apps to look professional. Luckily, his dad was a designer. Yuma shared his drawings with his dad and gave him strict instructions to make expert graphics for the apps. After approving the images, Yuma launched his first app, a kid-friendly calculator, at just nine years old.

Yuma: "I enjoy the fact that I can turn my ideas into reality by programming and making apps."

It was awesome! Yuma had coded a working app completely on his own. But since it still wasn't a game like the ones his friends enjoyed, Yuma kept working on his skills. The more he coded, the more he learned. By the time he was ten years old, Yuma had five apps available for download in the app store. He had even made some *simple* games, but he still wanted something more challenging. And he dreamed of inventing a highly successful, crowd-pleasing game.

Yuma applied for a scholarship to attend Apple's 2017 Worldwide Developers Conference (WWDC). If he could go to that event—one

PLAYGROUND FUN

Swift Playgrounds teaches kids and other beginners how to use the Swift programming language in a fun and interactive way. Users write lines of code to move a character through a virtual world. Robots, drones, and other characters teach kids the fundamentals of coding.

where even adults learned new coding skills—he knew he could figure out what he was missing.

The application required a sample interactive Swift Playgrounds project. Yuma dedicated three weeks to the creation. His final product included his own hand-drawn graphics in a find-the-bugs game. Players followed a virtual path from Yuma's birthplace in Singapore, through his home in Australia, and on to the California conference. Apple was impressed and chose Yuma for a scholarship. He was the youngest attendee at the 2017 conference, and the second-youngest person ever to attend.

On the plane ride from Australia to California, Yuma had an idea for a new app, a tip calculator that would convert United States dollars to Australian dollars, estimate the tax, and suggest a tip amount. Without it, he thought, his family wouldn't know what the US prices equaled in their own currency. Programming it took about an hour. Now feeling more prepared for his trip, Yuma spent the rest of the fourteen-hour plane ride napping and watching movies.

The next day at the conference, Yuma had the chance to share his design with Tim Cook, the CEO of Apple! Tim couldn't believe that a ten-year-old had created an app in only one hour. Yuma told Tim about his apps, all he had accomplished to that point, and his goals to go even further. Tim was blown away. So much so that he shared Yuma's picture and story in his keynote address to more than five thousand conference attendees, turning Yuma into an instant celebrity. Yuma ended up signing autographs and meeting developers more than three times his age who wanted to ask him about his process.

But Yuma gained much more than fame at the conference. In one of the presentations, he learned about augmented reality (AR). It sounded so cool to be able to put a cell phone game onto a real-life background! Yuma was hooked and began coding with the new technology as soon as he got home.

One of Yuma's previous apps had players stack blocks to create high towers. But it hadn't been unique enough. Now Yuma began working on an AR version of the game. Suddenly, the idea felt fresh and new! A player dropped blocks from a moving spaceship to build the highest tower possible. If the blocks didn't line up exactly, the sides dropped off, making the blocks thinner and thinner until a player missed the tower completely.

With real-world backgrounds, players could see just how tall their towers would be in real life. Could they stack their blocks taller than their little sister? Taller than their car? Taller than their house? The AR added a cool layer to the game. It was exactly what Yuma had hoped for. He finished coding the game in three months and named it "Let's Stack AR!"

Yuma prepared to upload his game to the app store and hoped this would be his big breakthrough. But right before his launch date, he found a bug in the game. Sometimes, as the block was falling, it would jump away from where a player had dropped it. But no matter what he did, Yuma couldn't seem to fix the bug on his own. He reached out to a software engineer for advice, but they couldn't help him either. AR was too new, so they had never seen a bug like it.

Yuma analyzed every single line of his code, but still couldn't find where the bug came from. He started to think that maybe it wasn't a problem with *his* code at all. Maybe the issue was with the AR framework (a base bundle of code that had been provided by Apple). Yuma changed the way that his game was written into the framework, and the bug seemed to disappear.

Yuma uploaded his game to the app store where people started downloading and playing "Let's Stack AR!" They loved it! But when the app updated, the bug reappeared. Yuma spent an entire year tweaking his code with every update. That got annoying

> In app development, a "bug" is a flaw in the program that makes it not work as expected. The process of finding and fixing the error is called "debugging."

fast. Yuma knew that he needed to find the true root of the problem. At this point, he was sure that the issue was in the framework. He compared the different versions of the framework and the operating system and finally found what was wrong with the code. A year after the game launched, he completely fixed the bug!

To top it all off, his friends played and loved the game! But they weren't the only ones. Apple featured the app as their Game of the Day, and people from around the world started playing "Let's Stack AR!"

Truly, Yuma had found something challenging enough to capture his attention—and with the ever-changing nature of technology, he would surely always have something new to master.

YUMA WENT ON TO:

- Create a YouTube channel to teach kids to code
- Share his story at global conferences
- Appear on television and in the news
- Return to WWDC every chance he got

PRODUCTION AND MARKETING

> Play the kid card! . . . People love helping kids. Especially those who are focused and ambitious.
>
> —Ehan Kamat, twelve-year-old inventor of the Solemender

So, you've finished an invention, tested it to make sure it's just right, and maybe even received a patent. What comes next? Well, many inventions are things you will use at home personally, or with your family and friends. No need to do anything else but enjoy.

Other inventions, though, might be things you want to mass produce and sell to the public. But how do you even get started with that? How do you get your invention into stores? How do you spread the word about a new product? Lots of the kids in this book had those same questions. And after lots of research and making the right connections, they figured out how to successfully sell their products. And you can, too, if that's the route you want to take.

DECIDE IF YOUR PRODUCT IS GOOD FOR SALES

First, you need to figure out if your invention is even something that people will buy. Getting a product to market takes a lot of time, work, and money. So if no one buys it, you will lose a lot of funds with no return. To figure out if people will want or need your product, you should:

Research potential buyers
- Who might be interested in your invention?
- Is there a need or want in the community for something like your invention?

Research potential competitors
- Is there something similar to your invention already on the market?
- Is your product unique enough to draw its own customers?
- Is your product an *improvement* on what's already out there?

Research where you might sell your product

- Would you sell in stores or online?
- If in stores, are the places you're interested in selling similar things?
- Will your product add to their supply, or compete with things they're already trying to sell?

FUNDRAISING

Once you've decided that there's a place for your invention in the market, you'll need to raise the funds to get there. And trust me— you'll need quite a lot of money. You might wonder why—aren't you about to *sell* your new invention? Aren't you supposed to *make* money from something like that? Well . . . yes. *Eventually*. But first you have to pay for things like materials, production costs, manufacturer fees, packaging, shipping, and more. All of that can take a lot of money. Luckily, there are plenty of ways to raise the funds. We'll talk about just some of them.

CROWDFUNDING

Crowdfunding asks for small donations from lots of ordinary people. Crowdfunding campaigns usually happen online with websites like Kickstarter, Indiegogo, and GoFundMe. But be careful, as most of these sites use an "all or nothing" idea. You set a fundraising goal and a time limit for the campaign. If you meet your goal in time, you get all the money at the *end* of the campaign. But if not, no one is charged, and you don't see a dime. With crowdfunding, backers help fund the product, and may or may not receive anything in return.

PRESALES

A presale is a sale before your invention is available for purchase. Unlike a crowdfunding campaign, money from a presale goes directly to you as it comes in, and you can use the profits as you go along. Presales promise buyers a product for ordering well in advance.

GETTING INVESTORS

Another option is to find investors—people willing to give you money to get your product or business off the ground with the expectation of eventually making a profit from your sales.

- Angel investors are private individuals who provide funds for a new company with the understanding that they will receive a percentage of the profits. Angel investors usually ask for a lower percentage return than venture capitalists.

- Venture capitalists are investors who work through a firm to invest in businesses and receive a portion of profits in return. They usually only invest in slightly more proven businesses. And they usually want a higher percentage of the profits than angel investors. They might even want a board position or a more hands-on role in the company.

PAY AS YOU GO

The pay-as-you-go method uses funds you already have to get started with a small amount of new product. Then you take the money you make from sales and invest it right back into the business to buy more materials and such. Using this method means you won't pocket any money for a while, but it also means you don't have to take money from anyone else or owe an investor a portion of your profits.

CHOOSING A MANUFACTURER

If you have the time, skills, and desire, you can keep making your product from home. But making enough to consistently sell and keep stock on hand is very difficult to do all by yourself while balancing things like school, soccer practice, and time with family and friends. So you might want to find a manufacturer—a company or person who makes products for sale.

To find a manufacturer:

- Research a few reputable companies that are proven and have made well-known products.
- Ask each one for a quote (that is, how much it will cost to make your product), compare their prices, and see which one fits your budget.
- Ask where they get their parts and make sure they use quality materials.
- Ask what their capacity is. If your business grows, will they be able to keep up with the work?

Once you've done your research, choose the manufacturer that best aligns with your vision.

DECIDING WHERE AND HOW TO SELL YOUR PRODUCT

A big part of bringing a product to market is deciding *where* you are going to sell it. Like everything else we've read about so far, there are lots of options! You'll have to decide which one is best for you.

STARTING YOUR OWN BUSINESS

Some people open a physical store to start their own business, and other people create a website or Etsy page to take sales.

Pros:

- You are in charge! No one else can tell you what to do with your invention or how to run your business . . . except maybe your grown-ups, of course.
- You keep most of the money from sales. You might have some costs in renting a shop or paying for a website, but those will be minimal compared with some of the other options below.

Cons:

- This option requires a *lot* of work. You will be in charge of managing inventory, taking money, organizing shipments, and dealing with unhappy customers.
- You will have to do all your own marketing.

Partnering with existing e-businesses. Instead of selling on your own website or Etsy page (and having to keep your inventory stocked in your own space and personally ship each item), you can partner with a business such as Amazon that will house your inventory and manage shipping in return for a portion of the profit.

LICENSING

Licensing means giving a business permission to produce, sell, and market your product.

Pros:

- The company already has existing customers who will see your product.
- The company does a lot of the marketing for you.
- You don't have to take care of the administrative side of things.
- You don't have to deal with shipping or managing inventory.

Cons:

- You only make a small percentage of the money from each sale.
- You may lose control of your product.

MARKETING

Once you've raised enough money to produce your invention, manufactured your product, and figured out where you will sell it, it's time to think about marketing—getting the word out about your product, promoting, and actually selling it. Marketing includes:

- Figuring out who your buyers will be and how to get the product to them.
- Creating packaging, logos, and a brand that will appeal to your customers—it's got to *look* good.
- Getting word out about your product. You might use:
  - » Social media
  - » Flyers
  - » Advertising in newspapers or on websites
  - » Word of mouth

Marketing is an ongoing process and can take a lot of time and effort. But if you want to successfully sell your product, people need to know it exists, where to find it, and how it can make their lives better!

There's obviously a *lot* to production and marketing. And we didn't even cover things like paying taxes, managing employees, or the nitty-gritty of going into business. Just know that if you decide to take an invention to market, it's not going to be easy. But think of the kids in this book who proved that nothing is impossible. If you want to sell your invention, don't give up! Take each step as it comes, do your best, and don't forget to have fun along the way.

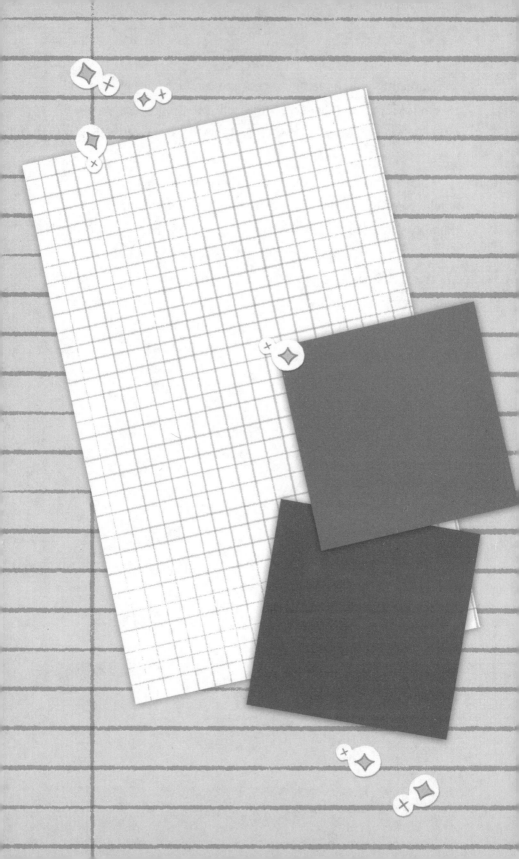

INVENTIONS FOR THE ENVIRONMENT

I've learned that you are never too small to make a difference . . . . I don't care about being popular, I care about climate justice and the living planet.

–Greta Thunberg, fifteen-year-old environmental activist and founder of School Strike for Climate

KEN LOU CASTILLO

MR. FUEGO

9 Years Old
Guatemala Department,
Guatemala
2005

Ken Lou Castillo loved camping out—sitting around an open fire with his family, singing songs or playing games in the flickering light, and cooking over the flames. But he always left feeling worse than when he came. Ken Lou was allergic to smoke, and all the fun events centered around the glowing fire caused an instant reaction. His eyes itched and watered, and his nose and throat closed up.

And it wasn't just campouts. Even getting warm near their in-home fireplace caused problems. But Ken Lou wasn't going to let his allergies keep him from important family activities or feeling comfortable at home.

Ken Lou also knew deforestation was a big problem in his home country of Guatemala. In the countryside especially, people could cut down as many trees as they liked. Ken Lou knew the people relied on firewood for both cooking and heating. So he set out to create an alternative to log burning. Something better for the environment *and* for his allergies.

Ken Lou and his dad experimented with different materials. At first, they gathered anything flammable they could think of. Paper, oil, even dirt. Ken Lou came up with the ideas and his dad made sure he stayed safe while experimenting with fire. With each new attempt, Ken Lou moved close to the smoke to see if it still triggered his allergy. Every time, it did.

And if that wasn't hard enough on his morale, Ken Lou faced another challenge. The other kids in his neighborhood thought he was weird for working on this invention instead of playing with them during summer vacation. When he wouldn't leave the project behind, some people called him stupid. Others told him he was wasting his time. Even groups of former friends started to make fun of him and bully him.

But Ken Lou still wanted to enjoy activities around a fire and help the environment. Instead of listening to the bullies and giving up, he listened to his parents, who always reminded him of how proud they were. He kept trying new formulas and eventually found a promising mixture of wax, sawdust, and wood shavings. But the

KEN LOU'S INGREDIENTS

Sawdust and wood shavings are the by-products left behind after cutting a piece of wood. The shavings are larger pieces while the dust is more powder-like. Both are often thrown out.

Wax is an organic compound that is solid but moldable at room temperature, and melts when heated.

first combination didn't make enough heat. The flame would never be strong enough to cook food or warm a large group. The ingredients were good, but the proportions were off.

Ken Lou spent another month experimenting until he finally found the right balance of parts. He mixed his formula and left the concoction in a mold to compress. When he brought it out to test, he saw the smoke it created was white instead of black—that was a good sign. Ken Lou smiled at the change, but still needed to know if it would trigger his allergies. He slowly got near and took in a deep breath. He waited for the watery eyes to come, but they never did. He didn't react to the smoke from his new log!

Ken Lou had finally solved his allergy issue, but even more important, his new invention was better for the environment. He had used recycled materials to make his log, and it burned for two full hours. It would take six to ten regular logs to last that long. It also put off 80 percent less carbon dioxide than traditional logs. And with only a tiny pile of ash left behind after a

Ken Lou: "Don't let anyone convince you that you're not capable or that your invention isn't worth working on."

burn, Ken Lou's log created 75 percent less pollution. He called his invention Mr. Fuego and trademarked the name, becoming the youngest person in Guatemala to receive a trademark.

> To import means to bring goods from one country into a different country to sell them.

But not everyone was happy for Ken Lou. He still faced taunting and bullying from the other kids. And now that he wanted to market Mr. Fuego, the harassment only grew, as many adults also became naysayers. They didn't believe a nine-year-old could market a product. Plus, few of them saw the need for a new kind of log. For their entire lives, the adults had been able to cut down any tree they wanted. It was easy, fast, and free. Ken Lou was asking them to rethink their way of life. He wanted them to consider how their actions were harming the environment and to pay for something that had always been free.

Ken Lou and his family didn't let the harassment stop them. They spent the next two years crafting Mr. Fuego logs by hand and delivering them to grocery stores throughout Guatemala. Eventually, other countries took notice and imported the product.

Once Ken Lou's product became widely recognized, some of his former bullies became his greatest customers. When one of the critics realized he had been wrong, he apologized for his behavior and offered to help take Mr. Fuego to the next level. He had an idea to create a machine to pack and compress the logs. The new device sped up production and made the process much easier. Ken Lou could focus more time on advocating for the environment and leave the log-making to the machine.

KEN LOU WENT ON TO:

- Be called the youngest inventor in Guatemala by news anchors and government officials
- Join the Guatemala Inventors Commission
- Receive the Erick Barrondo Order, which is awarded by the Guatemalan government to outstanding kids
- Appear on television to promote Mr. Fuego and educate people about deforestation

Whenever the theme song to his favorite show came on, Binish Desai couldn't help but sing along: *"Captain Planet, he's our hero. Gonna take pollution down to zero."* Binish watched the amazing Captain Planet, and a team of kid-heroes called the Planeteers, fight together against pollution. Binish wanted to be just like them. He saw the same environmental problems from the show in his own community. And he wanted to help save the world.

As he grew, Binish watched more and more trash piling up in dumps the size of mountains. He hated seeing the waste and asked himself what Captain Planet would do. He started looking for ways to reuse *everything* that would otherwise be thrown out. One day, as he watched steam spewing from his mom's pressure cooker, he realized that even mist could be recycled. Binish created a bowl to capture the steam, let it sit and return to a liquid state, then used it to water the garden. With this first invention, Binish realized that nothing needed to be wasted, and that everything in the world could be useful. This belief mixed with his curiosity and inventive spirit would serve him well.

When Binish was eleven years old, he heard a lot about the

difficulties faced by the poor in unsanitary and unsafe neighborhoods throughout India. Many people lived on the streets. Others had small homes made of only plywood and plastic. No one in these slums could afford to build a sturdy house. Binish knew that his theory about recycling could help these poor communities. He just didn't know how—yet.

One day, Binish accidentally sat on an old piece of chewing gum at school. That might seem really annoying or even embarrassing, but it actually turned out to be lucky. Binish pulled the gum off his pants with a scrap of paper, put the wad in his pocket, and forgot about it. But when he emptied his pockets that evening, he found that the gum and paper was as solid as a rock. Binish wanted to know why it had happened and if he could re-create it. If gum hardened so completely in the paper, maybe he could make bricks using the same idea.

Binish: "There is nothing useless in this world. What might be a waste to you is someone's asset."

Binish realized if he *could* invent bricks made from gum and recycled paper, he would be able to create a more affordable housing option for the poor, all while helping the environment. More motivated than ever, he got to work on his invention. First, he needed a spot to invent.

Inspired by *Dexter's Laboratory*, another favorite TV show, he blocked off a corner of the family living room to make a lab. He filled an old entertainment center with supplies and started experimenting, just like Dexter.

But his family discouraged Binish from following his dreams. They were well-known and well-respected in the community, and they worried that playing with trash would taint the family name.

PUBLIC INTERNET

Internet cafés let people come and use computers and the internet by paying a fee for the amount of time they spend online. These cafés are less common today but can still be found in developing countries where at-home internet is less widespread.

His parents tried to convince him to stop, but Binish was determined. He didn't care what anyone else thought. He was on a mission to save the planet and help the poor.

Binish made a small mold out of cardboard, about the size of a LEGO brick. He mixed chewing gum with paper his family had thrown out and let it sit in the mold. He found out that the mixture really did become as hard as a rock. The shape came out lumpy, flat, and more circular than rectangular, but it was hard and sturdy—Binish had invented a brick, using only recycled materials.

But since Binish didn't measure the ingredients, the bricks came out differently each time. He knew he needed a consistent formula and began testing different amounts and proportions of gum and paper. After four years of trial and error, he finally mastered his recipe. Every brick came out the same—smooth, solid, and well-shaped.

Binish started making full-sized prototypes of his invention. Once again, his parents begged him to give up the project. Hadn't he embarrassed them enough, they argued, spending years playing with trash? But again, he ignored their disapproval.

Luckily, Binish had one friend who was willing to help. Together, the boys made sure that the larger bricks were solid enough for construction. They hammered on each one, but none fell apart. They left them in water for days at a time, but they didn't disintegrate. They held them over an open flame, but they didn't catch fire. Convinced that the recycled bricks were strong enough, Binish moved on to his next task. If he wanted to truly make the invention useful, he needed to build something. He set a goal to construct an entire dollhouse.

There was only one problem—Binish didn't know anything about construction, even on a small scale. So day after day he went to a local internet café to read online articles about house building. He took notes, practiced at home, and slowly improved his skills. And by the time he was fifteen years old, Binish built a dollhouse using his gum-and-paper bricks! But many of his friends and neighbors laughed at the design. They didn't think his invention was worthwhile or useful. This time, it wasn't as easy to ignore them. After four years of criticism, Binish was beginning to doubt himself.

Rotary is an international service organization partnering with individuals and businesses to provide humanitarian aid around the world.

Luckily, Binish spent the next year studying abroad in the United States as part of the Rotary Youth Exchange program. When he told his hosts about his invention, they loved the idea. For the first time ever, someone encouraged him to continue. They even helped him get a patent and plan how to make the bricks even larger (about the size of cinder blocks).

Binish returned to India, confident in his abilities as an inventor. Though most of his family, friends, and neighbors still doubted him, Binish wouldn't listen. He didn't care what others thought anymore. He knew his invention was good and he knew it could help the community.

At sixteen years old, Binish found a company that was willing to donate the leftover ends that were cut off during their gum-making process and usually thrown away. Then he convinced a large office building to send him their paper trash instead of taking it to the dump. He mixed the recycled materials into bricks and used them to construct his first full-sized home. Binish had become a real-life Planeteer, recycling trash to save the environment and using the product to serve the community.

BINISH WENT ON TO:

- Build hundreds of affordable homes and outhouses throughout India with his recycled bricks
- Use recycled trash to make lamps and jewelry
- Appear on the TEDx stage multiple times
- Recycle more than two-thousand tons of trash
- Develop another version of the recycled bricks using discarded face masks during the COVID-19 pandemic

DEEPIKA KURUP
WATER PURIFICATION SYSTEM

13 Years Old
New Hampshire,
United States
2012

Every summer, Deepika Kurup traveled to Kerala, India, to visit her family. While she was there, she bought bottled water because the local water was contaminated—it could make her sick. She didn't think much of it for many years. But as she got older, Deepika realized not everyone around her could do the same thing. She watched people lining up to fill bottles from a community faucet that flowed a murky brown. She saw young kids dipping cups into rivers so dirty she wouldn't touch them, let alone drink from them. But it was the only water these kids had.

Deepika returned home and started researching drinking water. She was shocked to learn there was a global water crisis—that more than 785 million people didn't have access to clean drinking water. She suddenly realized just how lucky she was to have good water.

Deepika decided to fight the global water crisis by inventing an affordable, simple-to-use water filter. Now she just had to figure out how. Her research had taught her about a new kind of water purification system called Solar Disinfection, or SODIS. People using this method put water in clear bottles, then left them outside to disinfect in the sunlight. After 6 to 8 hours of UV exposure, the water was safe to drink. But if the sky was cloudy, it could take *two full days* to purify

WATER, WATER, EVERYWHERE,
BUT NOT A DROP TO DRINK

Though the globe is covered with water, less than
3 percent of that is fresh water. And more than two-
thirds of that is either trapped in glaciers, too deep
underground to access, or highly polluted.

only two liters of water. And most adults need three to four liters *each day*. Deepika knew there had to be a better—and faster—way.

Deepika dug deeper. She read hundreds of scientific articles and found an improvement to the process. Photocatalytic SODIS used a catalyst (something that speeds up a reaction) to make the process faster. But this method still had lots of drawbacks. The catalyst coated the inside of the clear bottles, blocking some of the UV rays, so the process was less effective. Plus, the catalyst got into people's drinking water, which was super gross on its own. But even more than that, without a strong binding agent, the catalyst eventually washed away completely, meaning the process wasn't sustainable. Because once the catalyst was gone, the bottles wouldn't work anymore.

With plenty of research in hand, Deepika set out to improve the photocatalytic SODIS system. She started running experiments in her kitchen. But her parents weren't thrilled about beakers of dirty water spread out over the countertops. After all, they had to eat in that room! So Deepika moved her lab to the garage. But before long, her project grew so big that she needed more space. She started prepping everything in the basement and moving beakers onto the deck to experiment in the sunlight. The project had taken over the entire house!

Deepika's first goal was to find a safe binding agent to hold on to the catalyst. If the catalyst stayed on, the filter could theoretically be used forever. She tried different spray glues and epoxies. But they were either toxic, making the water dangerous to drink, or too weak, washing away in the water. Deepika grew frustrated when the trials failed, but she refused to give up. Finally, she found a cement that kept the catalyst in place and was safe to use.

Deepika created three different prototypes to test the idea. The first was a cement rod coated with the catalyst that fit inside a water bottle. The second dropped small balls made with the catalyst and cement directly into the water. And the third was a series of tubes for water to pass through, filled with the same spheres from her second prototype.

Deepika filled all her filters with the contaminated water she had gathered from her local wastewater treatment plant. She set them out in the sun and tested the water after enough time had passed. It was clean! All three designs had worked. Deepika measured the contaminants in the water and found that the tubes filled with the catalyst spheres had purified the water best. In fact, it had reduced the number of total bacteria from eight thousand parts down to only fifty (a safe amount) and *E. coli* levels from more than one thousand to *zero*.

Deepika knew her invention could help fight the water crisis, but she needed to get the word out if she wanted to have any lasting impact. So she entered science fairs where she could tell the world about her water purifier. President Obama even invited her to the White House Science Fair where she presented her invention and discussed the global water crisis.

UV rays only make up about 3 to 5 percent of solar radiation. Visible light makes an additional 44 percent.

Deepika could have stopped there. After all, she had a solution that worked, but she knew her invention could be improved even more. Like other photocatalytic systems, it only harnessed UV rays, so the process was still slower than she would have liked. If she could harness *visible* light, the water would purify much faster.

Deepika went back to the internet and scientific journals and discovered that a chemical compound called silver nitrate might be the solution. She added it to her catalyst and ran more tests. After another year of work, Deepika finally figured out how to use the compound. Now the new catalyst did indeed harness visible light, making the cleaning process even faster.

But Deepika knew there were still improvements to make. She spent a third year researching and prototyping. At fifteen years old, Deepika realized she could make a purification system that *combined* her new catalyst with filtration. After dripping the water through a filter that removed 98 percent of the bacteria, it became 100 percent safe to drink after only fifteen minutes sitting in the sun. Deepika's invention took a two-day process and did a better job in only a few minutes. Without leaving any chemicals behind.

DEEPIKA WENT ON TO:

- Win first place in the Stockholm Junior Water Prize National Competition
- Be named the Young Scientist of the Year by 3M
- Speak on the TEDx stage
- Encourage people to advocate for change to combat the water problems in the world

KEIANA CAVÉ
MOLECULE TO DETECT TOXINS

15 Years Old
Louisiana,
United States
2013

Keiana Cavé could smell oil. Even though she was more than seventy-five miles away from the spot in the Gulf of Mexico where the infamous BP oil spill had happened, the fumes were in the air all around her. Keiana knew that couldn't be healthy. And then in her science class, she learned about photoproducts—dangerous substances that can be released from chemicals when they react with the sun. Watching the news, Keiana realized that no one was testing for these after the spill. She knew they were missing something.

But Keiana didn't know much about the photoproducts, so she wanted professional help. She emailed thirty well-known professors. She had no connections to them and had never met them before. But she hoped they would help her anyway. She asked if they knew anything about chemicals releasing after the oil spill. Twenty-eight of them laughed at her. They didn't think a teenage girl should get involved. Surely, they thought, she didn't understand what she was talking about. But two of the professors actually listened. They realized Keiana was onto something and told her what they knew about photoproducts.

One professor spent extra time with Keiana, encouraging her to

test for the substances. She taught Keiana good research techniques, like how to run an experiment, explore a hypothesis, and record her findings. Keiana spent an entire summer working at the University of New Orleans simulating oil spills, exposing them to UV rays, and separating the compounds. She discovered when the sun hit the oil, dangerous cancer-causing toxins were indeed released. But no one had ever discovered photoproducts after an oil spill before, or used her process, so Keiana needed to make sure her findings were right. She simulated *more than one hundred* oil spills. And the results held true. Keiana had invented a way to detect toxins in the water.

The summer of research excited Keiana. She wanted to do more, but her time was limited with many activities, from cheerleading to ballet, swim team to piano lessons. Eventually, she had to make a decision . . . She either needed to simplify her schedule or give up on the research. It was hard, but Keiana stopped participating in sports and music lessons to focus on her project.

When school started again in the fall, Keiana shared her findings with her teacher. The teacher was impressed and encouraged her to enter the project in a local science fair. Without a lot of time to pre-pare, Keiana threw together a homemade poster with snippets of her findings printed and pasted to a trifold board. Because her printer ran out of toner, half of the board was printed in blue ink and the other half in green ink. She didn't think it would matter at a local science fair.

But when Keiana got to the fair and saw the other participants, she gasped. They had their projects *professionally* printed on large, colorful boards. Keiana tried to avoid any attention as she put her makeshift presentation up next to the more official-looking projects. She apologized to the judges for her homemade board and sheepishly shared her findings. She left the fair certain she would lose. In fact, she didn't even attend the awards ceremony.

Instead, Keiana went to a nearby robotics competition. She was the captain of her team, so she didn't want to skip out on her responsibilities just to attend an awards ceremony for an event she had surely lost. So Keiana asked her mom to go to the ceremony in her place.

After the fun robotics competition, Keiana was surprised to get a call from her mom. She couldn't believe the news. She had actually won first prize in the science fair! But since she hadn't attended the ceremony, her mom had awkwardly accepted the award in her name.

With a blue ribbon in hand, Keiana went on to the state science fair, where her previous predictions came true. She didn't even place. Still, her win at the qualifying local level landed her a spot at the International Science and Engineering Fair (ISEF). Keiana prepared for the

Keiana: "Follow what you want to do no matter what. Maybe you don't look like them, and they might not think that you know as much as they do, but you have to prove you do."

event with a more professional project board. This time, she didn't have to be embarrassed standing next to the other participants.

Keiana enjoyed presenting, but after her experience at the state level, she figured she didn't have much of a chance at the international fair. She spent the awards ceremony scrolling through social media, trying to distract herself from what she knew would be a loss. But to her amazement, she took second place out of about 1,600 students from around the world! She quickly turned off her phone and walked down the aisle to accept the award. Still slightly in shock from the win, Keiana shook hands with the judges and smiled for the cameras.

The win helped Keiana know for sure that people cared about what she had been working on. With the confidence boost, she shifted her focus to *solving* the problem she had found. But she needed a bigger lab than the one she had at school. So she skipped her study hall hour every day to continue her research at Tulane University. Since it was only a five-minute walk from her high school, Keiana hoped she could slip out and back undetected.

But it didn't take long for her school to notice she was missing. The CEO (who sat above the principal and dean) called Keiana to her office. Keiana shook as she took the long walk, certain she was in major trouble. But the CEO surprised her. She only wanted to learn more about Keiana's research. When Keiana explained what she was working on, the CEO agreed to create a brand-new course so Keiana could continue the project—without skipping class again.

By the end of the year, Keiana had invented a molecule to stop the effects of the photoproducts that are released from oil spills. Her first invention had found that people were breathing in dangerous chemicals after the spills. Now there was a way to prevent those toxins from ever getting into the air to begin with. By asking questions that no one else had considered and testing ideas that no one else had imagined, Keiana invented a solution to a global problem before she had even finished high school!

KEIANA WENT ON TO:

- Have a minor planet (located between Mars and Jupiter) named after her as part of her ISEF prize
- Write academic papers describing both her method to detect toxins and how to stop the toxins from releasing
- Connect with Chevron, the oil company, who gave her $1.2 million in funding to continue her research and eventually bought her business
- Speak on the TEDx stage
- Be named one of *Forbes* magazine's 30 Under 30

ASUKA KAMIYA
SELF-SORTING RECYCLING BIN

12 Years Old
Aichi Prefecture,
Japan
2015

Asuka Kamiya always looked for opportunities to help her family. From baking her little brother's birthday cake to helping her parents around the house, she was always thinking of others. So when Asuka visited her grandpa's grocery store, it didn't take long for her to notice that one of his tasks was clearly no fun. He spent hours each week sorting aluminum and steel cans for recycling. It was hard to tell which cans were made of aluminum and which were made of steel without picking up each one individually.

Asuka remembered her grandpa's job when she was given a summer project to invent something brand-new in only two and a half months. Right away, she knew what she wanted to do. Obviously, recycling was important for the environment. But what if she could speed up the process and save her grandpa some time? Asuka set out to invent a self-sorting recycling bin.

Asuka thought her invention would come together quickly. She knew magnets would attract the steel but not the aluminum. So she assumed she could use a magnet to easily solve her problem. Her first experiment was encouraging. She put a magnet on the right side of the bottom of a piece of cardboard and slid cans down the left side.

The magnet drew the steel cans into a basket on the right while the aluminum cans fell straight down into their own separate basket. The experiment showed Asuka that her idea was good. She was sure the project was almost complete.

Asuka decided to craft a prototype of a two-compartment bin using the same ideas from her experiment. First, she made a divider that ran halfway up the center of a trash can. Then she made an opening for the cans at the top and put a magnet on the right side to pull the steel into its own compartment. But with the bin's opening on the left, the steel cans didn't get close enough to the magnet and fell straight down with the aluminum cans.

Asuka needed a way to get the cans closer to her magnet. She brainstormed new ideas with her mom. Being able to talk things out helped her visualize new options. And when she was out of ideas, Asuka's mom asked questions to help her move in a new direction.

Finally, Asuka came up with the idea of adding a small piece of plastic near the opening to guide the cans toward the magnet. She angled the plastic so that the cans rolled toward the center of the bin, hoping to get the steel cans close enough to the magnet for them to move to the right, but leave enough room for the aluminum cans to fall to the left.

Asuka finished the prototype and began testing with different

SORTING YOUR RECYCLABLES

Recycling requirements vary across the globe. In some places, people don't have to separate their own aluminum and steel cans. Instead, they are sorted in recycling plants using magnets and machines after pickup. But in other places, like Japan, people are responsible for sorting their own recyclables.

cans. After a few trials, she saw that the steel cans did move to the right of the bin. But now the magnet was a little *too* strong—the steel stuck to it without falling into the bottom.

Asuka added another small piece of plastic angled under the magnet. The magnet still drew the steel cans to the right. But the second piece of plastic created a barrier and a guide, directing the cans without letting them physically touch the magnet. This time, the cans fell into the correct compartment instead of getting stuck. It worked just as Asuka had hoped! But when she tried it again, it *didn't* work. What went wrong? How could her invention work sometimes but not every time?

Asuka ran many tests. She put can after can into her recycling bin and watched closely to see what was making the difference. She soon learned just how inaccurate the bin was. Sometimes it worked. But other times, the cans didn't go to the right side at all. And sometimes, they snuck around the second piece of plastic and stayed attached to the magnet without falling to the bottom.

The summer was almost over, and Asuka *could not* figure out why her results were different every time. She thought about giving up on her project, but her parents encouraged her to try again. They believed in her and knew she shouldn't quit. Her dad even helped to make new prototypes. This allowed Asuka to discover the problem. The plastic pieces were too short. If the top plastic piece wasn't long enough, the steel cans didn't always get close to the magnet. And if the second piece was too short, the cans could wrap around it and get stuck to the magnet above.

Now that she finally had an answer, Asuka was ready to solve the problem. She made three different bins with longer plastic pieces—three, four, and five centimeters long. She put can after can into the bins and recorded which length worked best. Finally, only five days before the end of summer vacation, Asuka found that a three-centimeter plastic piece consistently pushed the can to the right without leaving it attached to the magnet.

Asuka: "Try your ideas even if they don't work . . . I succeeded when I was about to give up."

Asuka took her working prototype to school. Her teacher loved it, and Asuka got a great grade. But even better, she was able to install the device in her grandpa's store and save him many hours of sorting metal cans.

ASUKA WENT ON TO:

- Receive a patent for her design, becoming one of the youngest patent holders in Japan
- Present her story on the TEDx stage
- Start a company with her dad to teach young inventors how to get patents for themselves

GITANJALI RAO
TETHYS LEAD DETECTOR

11 Years Old
Colorado,
United States
2017

Usually, Gitanjali Rao would try to eat her dinner as fast as possible so she could get back to her toys quickly. But one day, as she enjoyed her favorite pasta, something slowed her down. Her parents had the news on in the background and a story came on about the water crisis in Flint, Michigan. The reporters showed image after image of sick children. They reported that lead had gotten into the local drinking water. Gitanjali was horrified by the terrible pictures. But she didn't even know what lead was. Her parents explained it was a metal that had contaminated the pipes in Flint and poisoned the water. And lead poisoning was extremely dangerous, especially for kids.

Gitanjali couldn't shake the images she had seen. But what could she do to help people know if their water had been polluted? She had seen her parents use paper test strips. They would dunk the strips into water and colors would appear on the paper, showing if the water was safe or not. But when they lined a strip up with the color key to see if there were contaminates, the colors never matched. Her parents were left guessing most of the time. And water safety isn't something to guess about.

Gitanjali researched and learned that a more accurate option was to send the water to the EPA for testing in a lab. But that took forever. She knew that people who worried about the safety of their water couldn't wait for a lab to receive their sample, test it, and send the results back. Surely, she could come up with a better solution.

The Environmental Protection Agency (EPA) is a United States federal government agency working to protect the environment and human health. They enforce national regulations for clean air, land, and water.

A full year after hearing about the Flint water crisis, now ten-year-old Gitanjali read about a gadget that could detect hazardous gases. It used something called nanotube technology, which was new at the time. But if the technology could reveal the dangerous gases, Gitanjali thought the same principles could be used to find lead in water.

Gitanjali spent months studying everything she could find about the new technology—learning, reading, and sketching ideas. Combining multiple points from her research, she came up with a design for a 3D-printed testing box filled with nanotubes. Any lead in the water would bind to atoms in the tubes, and if she attached an Arduino board, she could code it to detect and read the results. Gitanjali understood how the principles of nanotube technology *could* work

SMALL BUT MIGHTY

Carbon nanotubes are microscopic tubes, thousands of times thinner than a single strand of human hair. They are incredibly strong. Nanotubes are unique because they can provide both structural support and work as conductors.

in her device. Unfortunately, the only prototype she had was a mock-up—no more than a cardboard box and wires to show where things would go.

Now Gitanjali just needed a little help to make her idea into a reality. Her teacher encouraged her to submit the proposal to the 3M Young Scientist Challenge—if she was chosen, she would be given a mentor to help guide the invention. But even with her teacher's support, Gitanjali didn't think she had much of a chance. There would be thousands of applicants, and other students would have *finished* prototypes, designs, and reports, while her project was still in the theoretical stages. But Gitanjali agreed to try, and sent in her project. To her surprise, she was actually picked as one of the ten finalists!

It all seemed like a dream—with an experienced 3M mentor, Gitanjali knew she could finish a real prototype. But she only had the three summer months to do it. So Gitanjali quickly connected with her mentor over video chats and phone calls to get the ball rolling. They brainstormed ideas and reached out to manufacturers to ask for nanotubes to use in their experiments. Things started moving in the right direction. Until Gitanjali's family decided to move across the country (from Tennessee to Colorado) that summer.

Suddenly, on top of preparing for the competition, Gitanjali had to help with packing and cleaning the old house. With potential buyers coming over, she couldn't leave her materials lying around. So Gitanjali spent every spare moment working and studying in libraries while the family got their house ready to sell.

Toward the end of the summer, when it came time to make the cross-country drive, Gitanjali packed as many supplies as possible into her suitcase. With more than a twenty-hour drive, broken up over a week, she knew there wouldn't be a lot of time to work on her invention. Though Gitanjali did her best to study and experiment in the evenings from the hotel rooms along the way, it wasn't nearly enough time to delve in as deeply as she wanted.

But there *was* a silver lining. The limited resources and hours spent trapped in a car gave her time to research more about the Flint water crisis that had started her quest. She read articles about real people who had suffered through the lead poisoning. With these personal stories in mind, Gitanjali felt even more motivated to succeed.

Gitanjali: "There are problems that we did not create but that we now have to solve."

When she finally arrived at her new house, Gitanjali gathered all her supplies and put together her first water-testing device. Using a specific kind of carbon nanotube that wouldn't dissolve in the water, she added different chemicals that she thought would react with lead. She crafted a disposable cartridge to dip into water and soak up a sample. This way, the device could be used over and over, only needing a clean cartridge for each test.

Gitanjali coded an Arduino to read data from the cartridge and send the results to an app she made for smartphones. She continued running tests and found that if there *was* lead in the water, the resistance in the nanotubes went up and the conductivity dropped. Knowing that, she coded the device to tell users if the water was safe, slightly contaminated, or very dangerous.

In October, just days before the final 3M event, eleven-year-old Gitanjali connected everything, dipped the cartridge into some water, and waited. Just as she hoped, the results showed up clearly on her smartphone.

Gitanjali called her invention Tethys, named after the Greek goddess of clean water. Not only did it work well, but it was faster and more accurate than any test she had tried before. Gitanjali won the final event and was named America's Top Young Scientist of 2017. But, more important, Gitanjali knew she was on the right track and soon no one would have to wonder if their water was safe to drink.

GITANJALI WENT ON TO:

- Make more improvements to Tethys
- Present at schools and science events, encouraging kids, and especially girls, to get involved in STEM education and inventing
- Be named *Time* magazine's first ever Kid of the Year in 2020
- Write the book *A Young Innovator's Guide to STEM* about her invention process to help other kids become inventors themselves

XÓCHITL GUADALUPE CRUZ LÓPEZ
WARM BATH WATER HEATER

8 Years Old
Chiapas, Mexico
2018

Xóchitl Guadalupe Cruz López was a lot like other preschoolers—full of endless questions and always wanting more answers than anyone could give. But unlike a lot of other four-year-olds, she had an opportunity to attend a new science program in her area. She got to learn things about STEM that she had only dreamed of. Xóchitl did lots of cool experiments with her teachers and finally found some of the answers to her questions. Soon, she was hooked on science.

After a year in the program, Xóchitl had the chance to do her first solo science project. She used flower scents to make an all-natural perfume that wouldn't hurt sensitive skin. The process was long and hard, especially for a five-year-old. But she stayed patient and persistent until she had extracted multiple scents from the blooms. Xóchitl won a blue ribbon in the state science fair for her work and was able to go on to nationals. She didn't win in the larger fair, but she didn't care. She had a great time meeting kids from all over Mexico and presenting her project to a group. It

STEM stands for science, technology, engineering, and mathematics. It's often used to talk about education and classes in these areas.

was so cool to have older kids and even adults listening to her. She knew she would be back.

But for her next project, Xóchitl wanted to invent something with more social impact. So she paid closer attention to the needs around her. One day, she watched her neighbors cutting down trees for firewood to heat water. Since they lived in a cold area, hot water was a necessity. But many of them couldn't afford water heaters. Xóchitl wanted her neighbors to have warm water, but she didn't want them hurting the environment to get it. And even though her own family had a gas heater, the bill was getting higher and higher, making it more of a burden on her parents. So Xóchitl set out to create a water heater that would be affordable and stop the wood-cutting.

Xóchitl sketched ideas in her notebook until she landed on one she knew would work: a solar-powered heater. She envisioned a box that would sit in the sun and warm the water inside. Excited, she raced to share the idea with her parents, but they had a hard time understanding. Xóchitl had worked so quickly that her diagrams and notes were messy and almost impossible to understand. Once she managed to explain the idea clearly, her parents started to believe she was onto something. They helped her gather recycled plastic bottles, hoses, and recycled wood to build her solar-powered water heater.

Xóchitl: "I learned that it's not always good the first time, and failures have to be taken as challenges to learn what we can actually do and not to surrender."

Xóchitl nailed the recycled wood together to make a box. She connected water bottles inside with hoses and tape. Then she ran more hoses from the base of the bottles to carry the water back out once it was warm. But her first prototype had many problems. The hoses leaked, spilling water everywhere.

The heater was too small and didn't hold enough water to be useful. And worst of all, the water didn't even get hot.

Some of these problems were easy enough to fix. Xóchitl replaced the broken hoses and added zip ties, connectors, and nylon to stop the leaks. She added more bottles, so that the heater held enough water to fill a bathtub. But the water still wasn't getting hot enough.

Xóchitl tried dragging the heater to different spots in her yard to catch the most sunlight. This helped a bit, but when she put her hands under the hoses, the water *still* wasn't as warm as she wanted. And if she didn't use it right away, it cooled down too quickly.

Finally, Xóchitl realized that the wooden box was making it hard for the sun to warm the water. She learned about the greenhouse effect and decided to swap some of the wood for glass.

Xóchitl found a broken refrigerator that had been thrown away and took out the glass shelves. She adjusted them to fit onto her solar heater and ran more tests. The glass created the greenhouse effect she'd hoped for. The water got hot enough and even *stayed* warm until she was ready to use it! Xóchitl named her invention the Warm Bath and prepared it for permanent installation.

Xóchitl wanted the heater to catch as much sunlight as possible but also be convenient for users. She studied the roof of her family's

RISING TEMPERATURES

The greenhouse effect is when greenhouse gases in our planet's atmosphere trap heat on earth, causing rising temperatures and climate change.

Xochitl's Warm Bath used the same principles, but without the negative effects. Her heater drew in and trapped UV rays under the glass. The heat couldn't escape, and the water temperature rose.

home and realized it got more sun than her yard. She found a spot that caught sunlight all day. But obviously, people wouldn't want to go up to the roof to get their hot water. So Xóchitl added hoses that were long enough to reach down to the house below. Some hoses would run water from an outdoor spigot up into the heater and others would send it back down into the house once the water was warm. Xóchitl attached the downward-flowing hose to a faucet so all she would have to do was turn it on when she wanted hot water.

When everything was ready, Xóchitl's dad hefted the large heater onto the roof. It was time to test if the invention would work once it was installed. Xóchitl turned on the garden hose and water ran up to the contraption. Once the bottles were filled, she waited until the water warmed under the glass, then ran it back through the additional hoses down into the home below. Xóchitl turned on the faucet and tested the temperature of the water. It was hot! In fact, after multiple tests, Xóchitl found it consistently reached 100°F to 120°F (37.8°C to 48.9°C)—plenty warm for a nice bath.

Xóchitl had made an environmentally friendly water heater out of recycled materials. She won another top prize from her regional science fair and this time went on to win the national fair. Over the next three years, Xóchitl crafted seven more water heaters for her neighbors and started on even more. Now they could have warm water without cutting down the trees, all thanks to Xóchitl!

XÓCHITL WENT ON TO:

- Receive an award from the National Autonomous University of Mexico for her work
- Become the first child to receive Mexico's Women in Science award
- Appear on television and in the news to talk about her invention

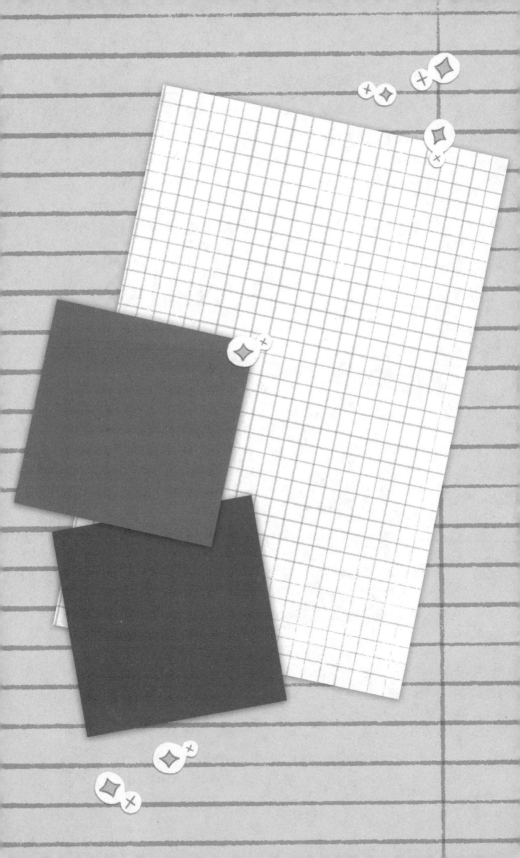

STEM COMMUNITIES

Get involved in community MakerSpaces . . . . It was through the science fair that I made some of my closest friends.

–Rachel Zimmerman Brachman, twelve-year-old inventor of the Blissymbol printer

When you come up with a new invention, you'll probably want to share it with others—after all, you worked hard, and people *should* know about it. Luckily, there are a lot of cool opportunities to connect with other inventors and scientists, share your work, and even get help to improve your own inventions.

SCIENCE FAIRS

Science fairs are cool! You get to come together to talk about projects that you've done using the scientific method. You can make a creative project board to display your findings. You will meet other kids who have similar interests and passions. You hear feedback from adult judges and scientists. And, often, you compete for a slew of awesome prizes.

Obviously, science fair projects don't *have* to be inventions. But . . . an invention *does* make a really great project! And as you've seen in this book, lots of these kids took the chance to share their own contraptions in local, regional, national, and even international science fairs! So if you have a unique invention, a science fair might just be the place for you.

Every region does things differently, so if you want to compete in a science fair, the best way is to ask your science teachers about specific opportunities in your area. They'll be able to point you toward school and local fairs. If you want to make it to one of the bigger national or international fairs, they'll help you find a qualifying event. And no matter what the outcome, you'll connect with other like-minded kids and have a blast doing it.

SCIENCE CAMPS

Science camps are great opportunities to spend time with fellow inventors or scientists. Kids come together to work on experiments, learn more about STEM, and develop innovations as a team and as individuals. Camp might be during the daytime or overnight, for one day or many days. You can find specific invention camps, programs focused on particular fields, or more generic camps that cover many elements of STEM. Check with your teachers to see which opportunities are available near you. Here are some fun camps to check out:

- **Camp Invention**, sponsored by The National Inventor's Hall of Fame (NIHF), helps kids learn about and develop inventions, and be inspired by the NIHF inductees.
- **Space Camp**, hosted by the U.S. Space & Rocket Center, trains kids like real astronauts. Based in STEM principles, activities include going on simulated space missions, creating and launching model rockets, and constructing Martian colonies.
- **The London International Youth Science Forum (LIYSF)**, hosted by the LIYSF nonprofit organization, is a two-week-long event where kids listen to lectures from international STEM leaders, present their own work, and learn how to use STEM in their daily lives.

HACKATHONS

Hackathons are fast-paced, exciting collaborative events where people develop new technologies. The goal is to create working software by the end of the event, which usually lasts only twenty-four to forty-eight hours. The events are so intense that participants sometimes don't even sleep as they try to race to finish their projects. Others catch just a couple hours of rest in a sleeping bag on the floor of their workspace.

Hackathons can produce general technologies or they might have themes (such as Music Hack Day, which focuses on sound technologies, and TV Hackfest, which develops television technologies). Others might be all about new cell phone apps, video game programming, or more.

Most hackathons are competitive in nature, and end with an awards presentation. One of the greatest aspects of a hackathon is connecting with people who have interests in the same kinds of technologies. Plus, the pressure of the time limit can be exciting and fun.

INVENTION CHALLENGES

Invention challenges give you an opportunity to create a *specific* type of invention. They're a lot of fun because they challenge you to think in a new way while giving you certain guidelines and parameters that you might not have thought up on your own. Here are just a few examples of these types of challenges:

- **The Rubber Band Contest for Young Inventors** is sponsored by the University of Akron's School of Polymer Science and Polymer Engineering. It challenges kids to make a new invention or art project *using rubber bands*. Kids have come up with things like a baseball pitching machine, energy converters, stretchy chairs, cat feeders, and more!

- **Kids Invent Stuff** invites four-to eleven-year-olds to submit their invention ideas for a chance to see them brought to life by adult engineers. No idea is too wacky—the grown-ups have made real-life version of things like a fuzzy car, a popcorn-blasting doorbell, and a robot crocodile lawnmower.

Kids send in a sketch of what they hope their invention will look like, and the engineers choose as many as possible to make and share the results on their YouTube channel.

- **The People of Play—Young Inventor Challenge** helps kids get their game and toy inventions in front of a panel of experienced makers. The event helps kids think up fun and unique ideas for sustainable, marketable, and playable games or toys with the chance to win prizes from toy companies like Mattel and Spin Master. Some entries have even gone on to get licensing deals from major game and toy companies.

LOCAL OPPORTUNITIES

Lots of the events and communities mentioned in this section are large-scale, highly publicized experiences. But don't forget about the groups in your own area. Maybe your school has a science club or a robotics team. Or you might check with your local library to learn about the STEM groups, classes, and programs they offer. Perhaps you can start a neighborhood invention club. There will always be like-minded people with similar interests who are ready to connect. So find your people and lift each other up, because there is truly nothing quite like community.

INVENTIONS FOR FUN

If necessity is the mother of invention, then play is its father.

–Megan Gambino, *Smithsonian Magazine*

FRANK EPPERSON
POPSICLE

11 Years Old
California,
United States
1905

Frank Epperson drank *a lot* of soda. But he couldn't grab a can straight from the refrigerator like we do today. In fact, in-home refrigerators didn't even exist when Frank was a young boy! Instead, most people had to go to stores called soda counters to get drinks from fountains that combined flavored syrups and carbonated water. Others, like Frank, made their drinks at home by mixing flavored soda powder into water with a stirring stick.

One day, Frank was outside mixing up one of his favorite drinks when he got distracted and left the cup behind. He spent a fun day riding in his self-made handcar and exploring with his brother, and completely forgot about his soda.

That night, the temperature dropped below freezing. The next morning Frank went outside to retrieve his cup and discovered the drink frozen to the stirring stick. He had never seen anything like it. Would the frozen drink be as tasty as regular soda? Frank grabbed

Before refrigerators for in-home use were invented, people used iceboxes, insulated containers filled with ice blocks, to keep food cold. Icemen delivered new ice to replace the melted blocks each day.

the stirring stick and pulled. A solid block of soda-ice popped out! Frank couldn't believe his luck and slowly took a lick. It was delicious! An accidental invention had been born.

Frank knew he was onto something big. He named his treat the "epsicle" (a mix between his last name and "icicle") and shared the idea with his friends. They loved it! But Frank lived in San Francisco where the temperature rarely ever dipped below freezing, so he couldn't make epsicles very often.

No one knows for sure what flavor that first ice pop was. Some think it was lemon, others claim it was cherry, and some even think it was actually punch instead of soda water. But the truth is, Frank never documented it, so any claims are simply best guesses.

Frank may not have had the resources to finish his invention as a kid, but he never forgot his epsicles. So once he was an adult, Frank looked for a consistent way to freeze the ice pops. Through his experiments, he learned that the mixture needed to freeze quickly. If not, the heavier syrup and sugar would sink to the bottom, leaving only frozen water on the top.

Frank made a container to hold test tubes filled with his liquid mixture. Then he surrounded the tubes with salt and ice, which is

COLDER THAN ICE

Salt lowers the freezing point of water. The normal freezing point is 0°C (32°F) but adding salt can drop it to as low as −21°C (−5.8°F)!

MORE FROZEN TREATS

The Popsicle wasn't the first frozen treat ever invented. In fact, ice cream had been around for hundreds of years before the Popsicle was born. But unlike ice cream (which is frozen in constant motion while stirred or churned), Popsicles are frozen at rest. Simply place a stick in the liquid and freeze.

colder than ice alone. With his new setup, the ice pops froze in only a few minutes!

But if Frank wasn't careful, the frozen concoction stayed stuck in the tube when the stick was pulled out. He found that the stick stayed in place if it reached the bottom of the test tube. So he put a weight on top while they froze to make sure the stick didn't float up. Problem solved!

But even when they were securely in place, Frank had more trouble with the sticks. Some types of wood changed the flavor of his ice pops, leaving a gross, sappy aftertaste behind. Frank's tests found the best type of wood for the sticks—birch or poplar, which were tasteless, sapless, and porous enough for the liquid to pass right through. Now licking the last drops from the stick was something to look forward to!

George Epperson, Frank's son: "I'll never forget how excited [Pop] was the day he learned his treats were selling well in Egypt!"

After a lot of hard work, Frank got a patent for his creation and began selling his treat at fairs, beaches, and rodeos. Frank's children

MADE BY A KID, SOLD BY HIS KIDS

Frank always included his kids in marketing the Popsicle. He got the treat into stores by sending his nine kids in one at a time to ask for the treat. When Frank went in a few days later, the store owners were glad to buy his ice pops after so many requests. Frank would also have his kids walk around amusement parks and beaches while eating a Popsicle. When other people saw so many kids eating them, they figured the treat must be delicious and tracked down Frank's stand to buy their own.

lovingly called his invention "Pop's 'sicle." The name stuck, and Popsicles spread throughout the world.

FRANK WENT ON TO:

- Invent lots of other things including a sunscreen, a powdered drink, and a dictionary organized phonetically, or by sound, to help people who couldn't spell well enough to navigate a regular dictionary
- Build two homes patterned after castles
- Sell his rights to the Popsicle, though the company still honors Frank as the original inventor

GEORGE NISSEN
TRAMPOLINE

George Nissen was determined to see the circus when it came to town, no matter what it took. At seven years old, he struggled under heavy buckets, bringing water to the elephants in return for a ticket to the show. It was worth it to see the trapeze performers. George was mesmerized by their act. As a gymnast himself, George couldn't believe the trapeze artists could perform such amazing stunts *in midair*. Year after year he watched them glide through the air, flipping, throwing, and catching each other before falling into a net below.

But the tricks always ended too soon for George, leaving him longing for more. The performers could surely keep going, he thought, if only there was a way to stay in the air longer.

George studied the trapeze artists closer. The net that caught the performers had just enough give to help them jump back to their feet. This small bounce at the end of a descent made George think that he could create something even *bouncier*. Something that would let performers spring back up to the trapeze bars high above and continue their tricks.

Around the time he was twelve years old, George had an idea to make his dream come true. He pulled the thick quilts off his bed

and hefted the heavy mattress to the floor. He took apart everything but the outer frame of the bed and stretched a single sheet over the remaining rectangle. George hoped that the tight material would propel him back up when he jumped on it.

But when George tried to bounce on the sheet, it fell to the ground, bringing George tumbling with it. He hadn't securely fastened it to the frame. This first experiment didn't work! And when his parents found his bed in shambles and his room torn apart, they weren't happy with the mess.

But George didn't give up. Even if his first prototype had failed, he knew the idea was a good one. He just needed a sturdier frame and better connections for the sheet. George spent the next four years searching for ways to make it work. He eventually used scrap metal to create a makeshift frame and strapped canvas to the outer edges, this time making sure it was firmly attached.

He tentatively stepped over the frame onto the fabric and jumped. The canvas sprung him into the air, caught him, and bounced him up again! At sixteen years old, George had his first working bouncing rig! He was excited, but knew he wasn't finished. This was a start, but his rig still was not as bouncy as he had hoped. There was no way it could launch acrobats back up to a trapeze bar.

George: "Inventing is one of the three things that make you happy. Working. Loving. And creating."

George finished high school that year and left for college where he shared his invention with his new gymnastics team. His coach and teammates loved his bouncing rig! Imagine the tricks they could do if they had more time in the air. The team helped George brainstorm new ideas and test different prototypes to find a better bounce. But one day, the new metal frame they tried collapsed on the first jump! Luckily, no one was hurt, and George realized that he needed to make a sturdier base. Eventually he learned that chrome plating the metal strengthened the frame enough to stop major accidents. But the mats *still* weren't bouncy enough.

Chrome plating adds a thin layer of chromium (a hard transition metal) over base metals. It increases hardness and provides greater strength.

George tried connecting the frame to the mat with strips of rubber from old tires, but the bounce still wasn't right. Eventually, after a few more tests and trials, George realized that adding springs created the rebound he hoped for, although they also needed to be chrome-plated for quality and safety. He knew he was getting close, but he still wasn't happy with the fabric used for the mat. Canvas didn't have a lot of give. So George tried different materials, searching for the one that would move best with the springs. He finally settled on nylon.

George found that weaving strips of material together (like making a tight lattice piecrust with vertical strips weaving over-under-over-under the horizontal strips) let air pass through the fabric and create

SEW BIG!

George had to use an industrial sewing machine to make his trampoline mats. It was the only thing that could handle such big strips of fabric.

NOT JUST A KIDS' TOY

The trampoline wasn't only an instant hit with children and gymnasts, but also for pilots in training. The United States government used the trampoline to teach their pilots to reorient themselves when falling through the air.

an even bigger bounce. Some designs left slightly larger holes for plenty of air—and therefore a bigger bounce. But the holes between the strips of fabric couldn't be *too* big, or toes could get stuck in the openings. George experimented with different weaves until he found the one that provided the best bounce *and* stayed safe.

Once he felt good about the material, George turned to experimenting with shapes and sizes for his bouncing rig. He made some rigs small enough to fit into the trunk of a car, and others large enough to fill entire rooms. He wanted to make something big enough to be safe, but small enough to fold and take on the road. Finally, he found the right proportions. After years of hard work, George had finished his bouncing rig.

But "bouncing rig" wasn't a very catchy name. When George traveled to Mexico with a performing team and heard the Spanish word for diving board—*trampolín*—he finally knew what to call his contraption. He added an "e" to the end, and the trampoline was born. He received a patent for the invention and trademarked the name before taking it to market.

George displayed the trampoline around the world. Always looking for the "wow factor," he became a star marketer. He demonstrated impressive gymnastic skills on the new device. He bounced on it with a kangaroo for a fun photo opportunity (even though the animal constantly tried to kick him). He even performed trampoline stunts on top of a flattened Egyptian pyramid to get international attention!

George Nissen's boyhood dreams ended up sailing higher than the trapeze artists he had long admired as the trampoline spread throughout the world. George's legacy still lives on today as people everywhere enjoy the same high-flying bounce that George dreamed of as a young boy.

GEORGE WENT ON TO:

- Use the trampoline to train NASA astronauts with a game called Spaceball
- Teach schoolkids about the invention process
- Receive more than forty patents
- Get trampoline events into the Olympics and even jump on the Olympic trampoline in Sydney, Australia
- Still be able to do a headstand at ninety-five years old

PETER CHILVERS
MODERN WINDSURFER

12 Years Old
Hayling Island,
United Kingdom
1958

Peter Chilvers always looked forward to summertime. Each day, he would spend hours on the water, sailing and exploring the island where his family vacationed. Sometimes he even built his own boats. Ones small enough that he could sail them alone. But they were *so* small that water tended to slosh over the sides. And sitting in a sailboat when the splashes came meant wet pants. Peter's soggy bottom was uncomfortable. Plus, wet pants could be very embarrassing. So Peter tried to think of a way to enjoy the sport while staying dry. He realized if he could stand while sailing, his problem would be solved—and a new fun sport would be invented!

Peter cut a large piece of wood and crafted it into a board with a pointed end. He took the sail and mast (the pole that supports the sail) from an old dinghy (or small sailboat) and attached it to his board. In a regular sailboat, the boom (or the sideways pole that holds the sail out) sits at the *bottom* of the sail and swings side to side so

Peter: "I wanted something a little different . . . I thought 'well, let's build something I can stand on and sail sooner than sit on and get my bum wet.'"

EARLY WAVE RIDERS

Although Peter's board is considered the first modern windsurfer, Polynesian wave riders may have begun standing on their boards as early as 1500 BC!

sailors could direct the boat with the rigging (or system of ropes and cords). But this traditional boom was designed for sailors who were sitting down, and when Peter tried to use it while standing, it proved quite tricky. If a strong wind created big enough waves, Peter lost his balance and tumbled into the water. Being completely drenched was even worse than having wet pants! So the first issue Peter needed to solve was how to steady himself on the board.

Peter created a wooden boom handle out of dowels tied together and experimented with passing it through the *middle* of the sail, rather than the bottom. He found that the new boom still worked well to steer the board, and even better, he could hang on and balance while standing. No more wet pants! But the new setup was hard to navigate, and Peter struggled to direct the board. If he was going to sail, and not just stand on the board, something else needed to change.

The sail on a windsurfer propels the board forward *and* helps the board change direction.

Peter realized that the sail needed to rotate a complete 360 degrees in order to steer the board any direction. This meant that he couldn't have any support pieces attached to the sail. Even though the rigging kept the sail up in a regular sailboat, it was limiting—the sail could only swing side to side.

SPEED ON THE WATER

Though the average speed a windsurfer can reach is 30 to 35 miles per hour, windsurfers have reached speeds of up to 60 miles per hour!

So Peter added a metal eyelet as a universal joint (a circular piece of metal that spins 360 degrees) to the center of his board. He screwed a hook into the bottom of his mast and connected it to the joint. Without any ropes, the sail now attached to the board, but laid on the ground until someone was ready to use it. Peter stepped onto the board, grabbed the boom handle, and lifted it to test his design. The sail, mast, and boom were light enough that he could support them on his own without any additional cords or wires. And the universal joint let Peter turn the sail in any direction to catch the wind.

Peter eased the board onto the water for his first attempt at sailing it around the island. He leaned forward and realized that the board turned away from the wind. He leaned backward and it turned into the wind. Soon he had the hang of it, and easily glided across the water while standing—without wet pants! Peter

Windsurfing became an Olympic sport in 1984.

had invented a modern windsurfer. His mom lovingly called the new invention a sailboard, a mix between a sailboat and a surfboard, and Peter enjoyed many days sailing around Haling Island.

Around the same time, others created similar sailing boards. Later in life, Peter would have to defend his invention and prove that he crafted his board at only twelve years old. Luckily, his neighbors remembered him windsurfing as a boy and could testify for him. He won his case, but the other inventors are often credited with bringing windsurfing to the masses. Still, Peter solidified his place in history as the godfather of modern windsurfing.

PETER WENT ON TO:

- Swap the wooden board for a fiberglass board
- Market and sell his windsurfer after various improvements
- Open a windsurfing and water sport shop
- Defend his rights to sell the board when others claimed patent infringement

HRIDAYESHWAR SINGH BHATI

SIX-PLAYER CHESS VARIANT

9 Years Old
Jaipur, India
2011

Hridayeshwar Singh Bhati played chess almost every day. And he was good. He loved playing with his dad, his friends, and anyone else who would join him. But when his chess-loving friends got together, only two of them could play at a time. Hridayeshwar asked his dad to buy a version that everyone could play together. When his dad told him there wasn't any such board, Hridayeshwar decided to take matters into his own hands.

It wasn't the first time Hridayeshwar had set out to solve a problem by inventing his own solution. Years before, he had been diagnosed with Duchenne muscular dystrophy, a condition where his muscles became weaker and weaker. In time, he couldn't walk at all, and instead used a wheelchair. People often told him that he wouldn't be able to do things for himself. But Hridayeshwar always invented a way. When he couldn't find a wheelchair that met all his needs, he crafted his own improvements. And when his dad had to lift him into the car, Hridayeshwar designed a wheelchair ramp so he could get himself in.

So, when Hridayeshwar learned that there was no such thing as six-player chess, he knew he could make it himself. He started by

Basic Rules of Traditional Chess

- The overall goal of the game is to capture your opponent's king.

- Each player takes turns navigating their pieces across the board in specific movements. If you land on a square with an opponent's piece, you capture that piece.

- Basic chess moves:

  - Kings can move one space at a time horizontally, vertically, or diagonally.

  - Queens can move any number of open squares horizontally, vertically, or diagonally.

  - Rooks can move any number of open squares vertically or horizontally.

  - Bishops can move any number of open squares diagonally.

  - Knights can move in an L-shape or 7-shape horizontally or vertically.

  - Pawns can move forward one square, or two squares if they have not yet moved. They are the only pieces that cannot move backward and the only ones that capture an opponent's pieces differently from the way they move. They can capture pieces on the diagonal in front of them.

- If a king is in a position where he could be captured, but can still flee or be protected, it's called "check."

- When a king is trapped, it is called "checkmate." Checkmate ends the game, and the player with the king that is trapped loses.

drawing three chessboards by hand and placing them side by side. But each board had 64 squares and trying to hand draw 192 total squares took a long time. If he didn't get them all the exact same size, the boards didn't line up and he had to start over. Sometimes the process took up to eight hours.

Hridayeshwar switched to a computer program that could make and save changes faster than the hand drawing. But there was a major drawback with the virtual designs. It was almost impossible to test the game without a physical board. Eventually, Hridayeshwar used a combination of both computer designs and hand-drawn boards to create prototypes. Once he liked an idea from his computer work, he drew it onto a physical board to test.

But his tests proved one thing. Side-by-side boards didn't work. They ended up being three separate games sitting next to each other. And Hridayeshwar wanted *all* six players to interact. So he tried hexagonal boards. After all, he wanted six players, and the hexagon had six sides. It made the most sense theoretically, but the shape

Hridayeshwar: "So what if I cannot move my body. I have moved the hearts of millions."

WHERE IT ALL BEGAN

Chaturanga, the precursor to modern chess, was invented in India. From there it went to Persia and finally to Europe before becoming the game we know and love today. Hridayeshwar enjoyed expanding on a game that had its roots in his own country.

caused lots of problems. One version looked good, but when he tested the game, the pieces all got stuck in the middle, unable to move. Other ideas got closer, but they broke the traditional rules of chess. And Hridayeshwar knew one thing for sure—he wanted his board to follow the official game rules.

Hridayeshwar finally realized that the hexagonal shape wasn't going to work and moved to a new idea using a circular board. But how could he create a circular board with the same number of spaces as a square board? Fitting squares into a circle either left gaps between spaces or cut some squares off. Either option made the board confusing.

Hridayeshwar saw that he couldn't use traditional squares for the spaces. Instead, he began testing rectangles with curved edges. He found a way to elongate certain squares and fan others out until they fit nicely in a ring. But the pieces were still getting trapped in the center.

Hridayeshwar needed to find a way for the pieces to pass through the middle without getting stuck. He couldn't add more game spaces because that would break the traditional chess rules. Each player could only have thirty-two squares on their portion of the board. Instead, Hridayeshwar crafted a center full of colorful triangles that worked as a passageway. The pieces didn't land on the middle spots, but instead followed the same color to the other side of the board, like an arrow pointing the way. Finally, no more stuck pieces!

Hridayeshwar was so close. But he still needed one last thing. Using the black and white chess pieces from his old game boards was really confusing with six players. Three people had the same color and it was difficult to remember whose pieces were whose! So Hridayeshwar crafted six sets in all different colors so that players could easily find their pieces.

After Hridayeshwar finalized the design, his dad helped him print the two-foot-wide vinyl game board. His own test runs had gone well. But now it was time to try the game with a full group of six players. Hridayeshwar gathered his friends and set up the large board. Each player easily navigated the board, even crossing through the center with ease!

Hridayeshwar and his friends loved finally playing as a group. But the board was so wide they couldn't easily reach the other side to move their pieces. So Hridayeshwar made one last improvement. He attached the board to a lazy Susan—a revolving circle that sits in the middle of a table. He and his friends spun the board for easy access to their pieces and it worked seamlessly. Now no one had to sit on the sidelines; everyone could get in the game.

HRIDAYESHWAR WENT ON TO:

- Receive a patent for his invention
- Invent twelve- and sixty-player chessboards
- Be named the youngest patent holder of India
- Receive awards from the Prime Minister of India
- Appear on television and in news articles

TRIPP PHILLIPS
LE-GLUE

9 Years Old
Georgia,
United States
2014

In third grade, Tripp Phillips was given a choice—either write a report or create a new invention. Tripp wasn't a fan of writing, so there was no question about it: He was going to invent something new. He asked his dad for advice, and his dad told him that the best inventions solve problems.

Procrastinating just a bit, Tripp started playing with his LEGO airplane. When the wing of the plane kept falling off, inspiration struck! Tripp could solve a problem *and* have fun doing it. He wanted to find a way to glue the building blocks together, but only temporarily so that he could use the bricks again in future designs.

Tripp's dad helped him contact the owner of a local glue company who taught Tripp the basics of glue-making and even gave him some supplies to get started. With a few powders to try, Tripp began to experiment by mixing different concoctions with water. When the powdered ingredients started to mix with the hot water, they quickly became sticky and hard to work with. Too sticky even to stir with a regular spoon. Instead, Tripp had to use a drill with a paddle attachment! This was difficult and definitely messy. Imagine holding a heavy drill over a large mixing bowl full of goop. But in the beginning, it was Tripp's only option.

While actually mixing the different glues might have been difficult, Tripp had a blast testing his experiments. Using each new concoction, he and his dad stuck new LEGO creations together, building and breaking, building and breaking, again and again. In only one week, Tripp found a working recipe. The glue held the building blocks together but dissolved in water so kids could reuse their blocks to create new designs. Tripp named his invention Le-Glue and never worried about broken block creations again.

But Tripp wanted other kids to be able to use his invention too. And if he was going to ask people to buy it, he needed to *prove* that Le-Glue really worked. Luckily, his dad was a scientist with a cool lab full of awesome gadgets. Using a machine called a tensile tester, they created an experiment to show just how strong the new glue was.

The machine pulled on the bricks and measured the reaction to the stress. With the machine set to the pressure that LEGO bricks can usually handle, the glue stayed firm. Tripp added more stress and the blocks *still* stayed together. He increased the stress again and again until he found that his glue made LEGO creations *ten times* stronger than the bricks were on their own. And Le-Glue still easily dissolved in water!

With proof that his glue worked, Tripp filed for and received a patent

STRETCHED TO THE LIMIT

Tensile strength is the amount of stress that an object can handle while being pulled or stretched before it breaks. Some things that undergo tensile testing are:

- Fishing line
- Rubber bands
- Garbage bags
- And of course, glue!

and went into business. But with orders stacking up, it was getting harder and harder to make Le-Glue by hand. Tripp needed help, so he decided to make his sister an equal partner in the business. They kept mixing the glue with a paddle drill and filling jars with Le-Glue using a baby spoon. The process was slow and tedious. Even with both of them working, they could only fill about thirty containers an hour.

Then one day, while slurping on an applesauce pouch, Tripp had his next great idea. Instead of putting the glue into a hard-to-use container, they could put it in a squeezable bag. He decided to use the money from previous sales to invest in the business and make packaging easier. He bought one machine that could mix the glue and another that funneled it directly into pouches. With these additions, Tripp increased production to five hundred packages an hour!

Tripp: "If you never set a goal, you can never meet a goal. So don't be afraid to take a chance, have a dream, and just try because it could come true. It does not matter what age you are, nine to ninety-nine, give your dream a chance."

Kids loved the product and added Le-Glue to all their LEGO creations. From airplanes to rockets, castles to pirate ships, their toys would never fall apart again.

TRIPP WENT ON TO:

- Win first place for inventions in the International Torrance Legacy Creativity Awards event
- Give "Tripp Talks" to schools and clubs to encourage young inventors
- Appear on *Shark Tank* at twelve years old and receive an $80,000 investment
- Make improvements to the Le-Glue formula and try new types of glue

JORDAN REEVES

PROJECT UNICORN: GLITTER-SHOOTING PROSTHETIC ARM

10 Years Old
Missouri, United States
2016

Jordan Reeves always sparkled and shined. Her mom said she had a special twinkle in her eyes from the time she was born that followed her everywhere she went. And Jordan went *everywhere*. Softball games, dance class, swimming meets, Girl Scouts, piano lessons, and summer camps all kept Jordan very busy.

On top of all her activities, Jordan loved to create. She was always looking for a chance to add her own unique style and flair to her outfits, school projects, and more. That was especially true when she had the opportunity to help design her own prosthetics.

A prosthetist is someone who makes artificial limbs.

Jordan had been born with a limb difference—her left arm stopped growing just above the elbow. She often preferred to leave her smaller arm as it was, but sometimes, if she didn't use a prosthetic (or helper arm as she liked to call it), she could overwork and injure her shoulder.

So Jordan took an active role in crafting each helper arm. That way, even on days she didn't want to wear one, Jordan knew it would

look amazing. She worked closely with Mr. David, her prosthetist, to make sure each one fit comfortably. But the fun really began when she chose a special design for each helper arm. Some were covered in princess pictures, some had kittens, and others used fun patterns, bright colors, or sparkles.

Since she was so experienced in designing her helper arms, Jordan was ready when the chance came to attend Superhero Cyborg camp. Each camper would partner with an engineer to create their own prosthetic limbs. The counselors explained that each child would come up with their own superhero alter ego, then develop a prosthetic to match their new persona. It didn't take Jordan long to plan. She dubbed herself "Glitter Girl" and started working on a glitter-shooting arm.

The camp was only five days long, and Jordan needed a working prototype to share at the end. When she learned about computer-assisted design (CAD), she knew the technology could help finish the invention within the time limit.

But first, Jordan created a simple prototype with craft materials and a plastic glove full of glitter to visualize the idea. It was cool, but she soon realized that the glitter shooter didn't need to look or work like a hand and started considering other designs.

Jordan sketched out a new idea, then 3D printed a round cuff

COMPUTER-ASSISTED DESIGN

CAD creates precise, clean designs. It lets you see and work in 3D. Though it does take more training than drawing does, the final project contains much more detail than a hand drawing can.

that would slide onto her small arm. Then she cut the tips from Nerf darts, filled them with glitter, and attached them to air puffers (small devices that push air out when you squeeze). She added a pull string to each puffer and glued them onto the cuff. When she tugged on the strings, air pushed the glitter out. But the round cuff wasn't stable enough. Plus, it was a pain to pull so many strings.

Jordan tried a star formation next, with six spokes jutting off the cuff and holding five air puffers tightly in place. That provided much better support. Then Jordan wove a single string around and through each puffer so that they released much easier with just one pull. She named the invention Project Unicorn for its sparkly fun.

On the final day of camp, Jordan shared her device with the entire camp. She pushed her nerves aside and pulled on the string, anticipating a blast of glitter greeting wild cheers from the crowd. But instead, glitter barely puffed out and onto the ground. The presentation had been fun, and people seemed to like her invention, but Jordan couldn't help but feel a bit disappointed as she walked off the stage. The camp was over and all she had was a trickle of glitter.

But if Jordan had learned anything in the last five days, she knew that failure was part of the invention process. She started to think about all she *had* accomplished. She had created a working prototype

A BIG BURST OF AIR

Compressed air forces air molecules into a small space. When they are released, they can move objects forward. Think of blowing up a balloon and letting it go without tying it.

in less than a week! And had a lot of fun doing it. Imagine what she could do with more time.

Luckily, Jordan returned home to learn that each camper would be paired with a mentor to help them finalize their inventions. She began working with Sam Hobish, an industrial designer who had taken an interest in Project Unicorn. They met every week over video chat to brainstorm new ideas. Their first goal was to find a way for the glitter to blast out *powerfully*. They tried using CO_2 first. It definitely created the bang they wanted . . . but it was a bit *too* powerful. The explosion of glitter could hurt someone.

Jordan and Sam tried using compressed air instead. This time, it was just right! The glitter blasted from the prosthetic but wasn't powerful enough to cause harm.

Since Jordan didn't have her own 3D printer, Sam had to print their design and mail it to Jordan to test. It shot glitter well, but she still didn't love the overall look. And once again, time was short. Jordan had been invited to present her invention at Maker Faire Bay Area (an event in San Francisco where experts and beginners get together to share what they've made) and only had a few weeks before the event. She kept thinking up new ideas until inspiration hit. Why not make Project Unicorn *look* like a unicorn horn?

Jordan and Sam crafted a new design—a long unicorn horn that attached to Jordan's small arm. It looked amazing! And they finished it in time to leave for San Francisco. But their troubles weren't over yet. Just before their presentation, Jordan realized the glitter she had been using was too big for the new design. It got caught in the horn. They searched many stores until they found a glitter fine enough to power through the horn, right in time to present at the fair! Project Unicorn was a big hit. After showing off the invention onstage, attendees clamored for a chance to be blasted with glitter. Jordan loved how happy her invention made people.

Still, Jordan wasn't finished making improvements. But now she wouldn't have to wait for Sam to mail her the printed designs. Autodesk, the company Sam worked for, and Dremel, a power tool company, had teamed up to give Jordan her very own 3D printer! With donated filament (the plastic used in the printer), Jordan set out to make final adjustments. Her current design used small vials filled with glitter for a single blast. And refilling the tiny containers was a pain. So Jordan developed a special compartment to hold enough glitter for multiple uses.

Jordan: "Some of my best prototypes came out of previous models that weren't working right . . . If you create something without failure, you probably need to keep working on it to make it better."

As Jordan's fame spread, a new issue came to her attention. People who had seen Project Unicorn on the internet and at the Maker Faire kept sending Jordan the same feedback: Glitter was bad for the environment. The traditional glitter she had been using was made with microplastics that would take thousands of years to degrade. Jordan didn't want that! She partnered with BioGlitz, a company that makes a biodegradable glitter proven safe for the environment and wildlife, and only used their products from then on. Now Jordan was a true superhero—spreading sparkles of joy *and* protecting the environment.

JORDAN WENT ON TO:

- Appear in viral internet videos
- Present at the National Maker Faire
- Appear on television and in the news
- Win the Dream Big, Princess innovator award from Disney
- Consult with Mattel about their first Barbie with a limb difference
- Co-author the book *Born Just Right* with her mom, to tell the story behind Project Unicorn

ALEX BUTLER
TACO VS BURRITO GAME

7 Years Old
Washington,
United States
2018

Alex Butler loved games. His *whole family* loved games. In fact, on family vacations, they didn't just sightsee or relax by the pool—they played a new game every day of the trip. Alex especially enjoyed strategy games. And he wanted to win. He became so good that his parents could rarely beat him.

By the time he was seven years old, Alex had played more games than many adults play in their lifetimes. And now he wanted to invent his own. A name struck him almost instantly—Taco vs Burrito. He had no idea how to play the game yet. But with such a cool name, he knew he couldn't go wrong.

Alex told his mom about the idea. She wanted to help and came up with a game that matched the name. She created a War-style card game where taco toppings worth the most points won the cards worth fewer points. She showed Alex and they tried the new idea. But after playing for an hour, they had to give up. There was no way to win the game! It would never end. Alex thanked his mom for her help but decided *he* should take the lead on game development after that.

So Alex got to work. He played games like Exploding Kittens,

Sleeping Queens, and Sushi Go! looking for what worked and what didn't work in each one. He studied the balance of cards in his favorite games, the rules of the most successful games, and the eye-catching graphics of the most popular games. But Taco vs Burrito still needed an end goal. And Alex finally had an idea. Build the wackiest, wildest, biggest meal to win.

Alex brainstormed every gross food he could think of to create these silly meals. Old broccoli, hot yogurt, and chocolate-covered shrimp all made the cut. Players would use the yucky foods to fill their choice of a taco or burrito.

But it wasn't enough to just build a meal. Alex needed another layer to increase the difficulty level. Cards like the Health Inspector and Tummy Ache took away a player's hard-earned points. Trash Panda cards could get those points back. And Crafty Crow cards stole cards (and points) from opponents. The game came together piece by piece.

Alex used computer clip art to design sample cards that he printed out on paper so he could begin testing his game. Every weekend, he and his mom visited their local coffee shop. They first played a round of one of their favorite games. They talked about what they loved about the game and how the strategy worked.

Then they played a round of the current version of Taco vs Burrito to see how it compared. Alex bounced ideas off his mom and other opponents to see what should stay in the game and what needed to change.

Some weeks, Alex made minor adjustments. Maybe he needed a better graphic for a certain card. Or to change a point value. Or to tweak a card's description. But some weeks, he needed to make bigger changes.

Alex spent many weeks tackling card balance. Too many of one type would sway the game unfairly. Not enough and the game wouldn't work. He figured out the right proportions and continued playtesting. Then he got rid of some cards that were too powerful and tested new cards in their place. After six months of this pattern, five complete overhauls of the game, and small weekly tweaks, Taco vs Burrito was finished. Alex used a prototype website to create a few sample versions of his game.

Alex shared Taco vs Burrito with his friends, and they loved it! But that wasn't enough for Alex. He and his mom started searching for a manufacturer to print the game in bulk. But every company they considered in the United States required a huge minimum order, and Alex didn't think he would sell enough to meet those demands.

So he looked to manufacturers in China. His mom got quotes from each one and made a list of all the places she felt would treat Alex with excitement and respect. Finally, Alex chose BangWee Games because he loved their name!

But to afford mass production, Alex needed more money. He launched a crowdfunding campaign, thinking he could raise enough to print and sell a few games and have a lot of fun doing it. Alex offered each financial backer a copy of the game. He filmed a video to introduce himself as a seven-year-old game inventor and launched the campaign.

Alex: "Try multiple things. If one thing doesn't work for you, try something else."

Alex's dad wanted to be his first donor, thinking that if nothing else, Alex would have at least one backer. But he was too late. In the two minutes it took his dad to log on to the computer, Alex's game had already gotten backers. People loved the concept of Taco vs Burrito and support came flooding in. The project was fully funded in only three hours! And by the end of the campaign, they had 697 total orders, blowing their original goal out of the water!

Alex sent the final order into his manufacturer and anxiously

ONE FUN JOB

Playtesting is the process of making sure all the bugs are worked out of a game before it goes to market. Some game developers ask for volunteers to try the game and point out issues, while other companies pay game testers. And some do both! The process of playtesting is common in both board games and video games.

waited. Once the games arrived, he packaged and shipped them to everyone who participated in the crowdfunding campaign. That took a lot of work and *a lot* of tape! But it was worth it. Everyone loved the game! People got so into it that kids had Taco vs Burrito–themed birthday parties, adults gave the game as gifts, and stellar reviews came in. Soon, more and more people wanted to get their hands on Taco vs Burrito. So many people bought the game that Alex's parents quit their day jobs to go to work for him! Now, that's good strategy!

ALEX WENT ON TO

- Present Taco vs Burrito at the Emerald City Comic Con event
- Partner with Amazon to stock, sell, and ship Taco vs Burrito, making $1 million in the first year and $3.5 million in the second year
- Create and sell expansion packs for Taco vs Burrito
- Invent more games, including Bold Made, a modern twist on the classic Old Maid

BE AN INVENTOR!

Nothing is more satisfying than thinking of something, designing it, and then having it work.

−Adia Bulawa, sixteen-year-old inventor of exercise equipment for astronauts

As you've seen in this book, kids can do amazing things—and you can too! If you are inspired to invent, create, and solve problems, here are a few steps for you to follow:

NOTICE A PROBLEM

- Observe. Ask yourself what needs to change or how something could be better.

  This might be something very serious like the need to decrease greenhouse gas emissions. Or it might be something fun like your need to hold your soda and snacks while still playing your favorite video game.

ASK QUESTIONS

- How can you fix the problem?
- What could make it better?
- Who would your invention help?

RESEARCH AND BRAINSTORM IDEAS

- See if anyone has had the same question before and how they answered it. Could you make their ideas even better?
- Look for ways to solve the problem. Make a list of ideas and choose one that you want to try.
- Draw a design and picture how your invention will work.

CREATE A PROTOTYPE

- Make a list of materials you'll need.
- Gather supplies and build a model of your invention. Ask for help if you can't do it all on your own. Family

members, friends, teachers, and neighbors might have the skills that you need.

TEST YOUR INVENTION

- Try your invention many times and record the results.
- Does your invention *consistently* do what you wanted it to do? If it does, great! If not . . .

TRY AGAIN

- Go back to the drawing board. Ask new questions. Try and test new ideas.
- Repeat the process over and over until you create a working prototype.

IMPROVE YOUR INVENTION

- Work out the small bugs.
- How could it be even better? What things would you change?
- Does your invention *look* like you want it to? How could you improve the design?

LAUNCH YOUR DESIGN

- Use your invention to solve your problem.
- File for a patent if you want to protect your idea and get a trademark if needed.
- Distribute your invention. This could be sharing it freely, taking it to science fairs, or going into business. Every invention is worth sharing with others in some way.

If you do your best and never give up, you'll be on the same path as the 35 amazing kids in this book. And who knows? Maybe *you'll* be the next great kid inventor!

GLOSSARY

alloy: A mix of two or more metals.

app (short for application): Software with a specific function or purpose that can be downloaded on a smartphone, computer, tablet, or other electronic device.

Arduino board: A microcontroller that can receive input and convert it to an output.

artificial intelligence (AI): Computer programming that allows machines or robots to complete tasks that usually require human intelligence, including decision-making and problem-solving.

biodegradable: Able to be naturally decomposed by bacteria or other living things.

catalyst: Something that speeds up a chemical reaction.

chemical compound: A chemical substance made up of two or more elements connected with chemical bonds.

chemical energy: Energy produced from a chemical reaction.

circuit board: A thin board that connects electronic parts.

code: Programming language that's understood by a computer.

computer-assisted design (CAD): The use of computer software to create precise, clean designs. It generally pairs with 3D printing for development.

conditionals: A coding concept that relies on if/then statements: *If* something is true, *then* the outcome runs.

consumer: A person who buys a product or service.

crowdfunding: Raising money through small donations from many people, usually online.

design patent: Protects new designs of previously existing inventions. *See also* invention/utility patent; patent; provisional patent.

diagram: A drawing that represents an idea.

diode: An electronic component that allows electricity to flow in just one direction.

distribution: Sending a product through the marketplace to prepare for sales.

durometer: Hardness level.

electrical energy: Energy that is created from the movement of electrons.

electrode: A conductor by which electricity enters or leaves a device.

electrolyte: The substance that stops a chemical reaction from happening too early in a battery and allows electrons to flow from one side to the other, powering a device along the way.

electrons: Negatively charged subatomic particles that create electricity when they move from atom to atom.

engineering: A branch of science that designs, builds, or invents something to solve a problem.

entrepreneur: Someone who starts and manages a business.

functions: Sets of code combined under one name. To run all the steps in a function, a coder simply has to call on the name of the function.

greenhouse effect: Trapped warmth from the sun.

hypothesis: An educated guess at an outcome. Hypotheses are tested and proved true or false.

inductee: Someone admitted into an organization.

injection molding: Filling a mold with melted material and allowing it to cool and solidify into a solid design.

innovation: A brand-new product, idea, invention, service, or creation.

invention/utility patent: The most common type of patent. Protects new inventions. *See also* design patent; patent; provisional patent.

investor: Someone who provides money to support a new business in the hope of earning a greater profit.

licensing: Giving a company permission to sell a product.

manufacturer: A company that produces goods for sale.

market: To promote and advertise.

mechanical energy: Energy created from motion.

microcontroller: A small electronic circuit that holds multiple electronic components and connections that can control some of or all of an electronic device.

molecule: A group of atoms held together by chemical bonds.

patent: A document that protects your invention. With a patent, no one else can legally produce the invention for up to twenty years. *See also* design patent; invention/utility patent; provisional patent.

pitch: A presentation to persuade others to buy or invest in a product.

pro bono: Free of charge.

product: An item made to sell.

production: Making or manufacturing a product.

programming: Designing a computer program to complete a certain task.

prototype: Early attempts at an invention. Prototypes can range from rough ideas to fully functional designs.

provisional patent: Gives applicants the time to complete a full utility patent. Deems an invention "patent pending." *See also* design patent; invention/utility patent; patent.

resistor: An electrical component that limits the flow of electricity.

retailer: Someone who sells goods or services.

robotics: The use of a mix of engineering and computer science to design, build, program, and operate robots.

sequences: In computer code, a set of steps that has to run in a certain order.

soldering: The process of joining two pieces of metal together using a metal alloy known as solder as a filler piece. You put the solder between the two ends, heat the filler up until it melts, then let it cool until it hardens, and the two metals are connected.

STEM: Acronym for science, technology, engineering, and mathematics.

thermoplastics: Plastics that melt under heat but return to solid when cooled.

trademark: Legal protection of a name, brand, logo, symbol, phrase, etc.

transistor: A small electronic device that regulates the flow of electricity and serves as an on/off switch.

ultrasonic sensor: A device that measures distance by sending out sound waves and measuring the amount of time it takes for the waves to bounce back.

utility model: Similar to a patent but offers less protection for a shorter time. Often used for rapidly changing areas of invention. Not available in the United States.

QUOTE SOURCES

p. v—Prisha Shroff

Torres, Jorge. "Valley Teen Inventor Earns Distinguished Honor." *ABC 15 News*, last modified June 24, 2022, https://www.abc15.com/news/uplifting -arizona/valley-teen-inventor-earns-distinguished-honor.

p. 1—Kid President

Novak, Robby. "How to Be an Inventor! Kid President." Uploaded by Soul-Pancake, February 9, 2014. YouTube video, 2:34. https://www.youtube .com/watch?v=75okexRzWMk.

p. 3—Benjamin Franklin

Franklin, Benjamin. *The Autobiography of Benjamin Franklin*. United Kingdom: P F Collier and Son, 1909, pp. 116–117. Google Books, https:// www.google.com/books/edition/The_Autobiography_of_Benjamin _Franklin/Mi0LAAAAIAAJ.

p. 9—Louis Braille

Mellor, C. Michael. *Louis Braille: A Touch of Genius*. Boston: National Braille Press, 2006.

p. 16—Kathryn "KK" Gregory

Gregory, Kathryn. "About KK Gregory, Inventor of Wristies®" Wristies. https://www.wristies.com/KK_Wristies_Inventor_s/152.htm. Accessed January 25, 2021.

p. 20—Richie Stachowski

"Richie Stachowski: Water Talkies™." Massachusetts Institute of Technology. https://lemelson.mit.edu/resources/richie-stachowski. Accessed January 27, 2021.

p. 27—Karoli Hindriks

Email interview. Conducted by Kailei Pew, January 18, 2022.

p. 32—Cassidy Goldstein

"Cassidy Is Named Inventor of the Year." Intellectual Property Organization Inventor of the Year 2006. Uploaded by IdeaLocker, September 29, 2009. https://www.youtube.com/watch?v=6BYzGMyRzus.

p. 39—Sofia Overton

Overton, Sofie. "WisePocket Indiegogo v2." January 18, 2018. YouTube video, 3:28. https://www.youtube.com/watch?v=7BdrD9g_Ow0.

p. 41—Temple Grandin

Grandin, Temple with Betsy Lerner. *Calling All Minds: How to Think and Create Like an Inventor.* New York: Puffin Books, 2018, p.7.

p. 51—Mark Leschinsky

Email interview. Conducted by Kailei Pew, February 2, 2021.

p. 54—Spencer Whale

Wolf, Theo. "Coach Profiles: Introducing Spencer Whale." Spike Lab, May 7, 2020. https://spikelab.com/coach-profiles-introducing-spencer-whale/.

p. 62—Remya Jose

James, T. J. "Washing Cum Exercise Machine." National Innovation Foundation of India. https://nif.org.in/upload/innovation/3rd/312-washing-cum-exercise-machine.pdf.

p. 67—Lily Born

Born, Lily. "Kangaroo Cup Kickstarter Video 2014." Uploaded by Joe Born, June 18, 2014. YouTube video, 2:34. https://www.youtube.com/watch?v=bKhrEH0rhcg.

p. 72—Maria Vitória Valoto

Valoto, Maria Vitória. "Como a educação salvou minha vida." TEDxLaçador. Uploaded by TEDx Talks, June 18, 2019. YouTube video, 12:03. https://www.youtube.com/watch?v=1eSRhD1Kii8.

p. 77—Bishop Curry V

Curry, Bishop. "I Don't Think Babies Should Die in Hot Cars." TEDxPlano. Uploaded by TEDx Talks, April 18, 2018. YouTube video, 9:09. https://www.youtube.com/watch?v=l1XKRpBRZJA.

p. 85—Cassidy Crowley

Crowley, Cassidy. "Cassidy Crowley Talks About Inventing the Baby Toon." Uploaded by The Baby Toon, February 28, 2020. YouTube video, 1:10. https://www.youtube.com/watch?v=8RO70HUkNcA.

p. 88—Dasia Taylor

Machemer, Theresa. "This High Schooler Invented Color-Changing Sutures to Detect Infection." *Smithsonian Magazine*, March 25, 2021. https://www.smithsonianmag.com/innovation/high-schooler-invented -color-changing-sutures-detect-infection-180977345/.

p. 92—Shakeena Julio

"Autodesk and Makeosity." Uploaded by Autodesk Education, April 7, 2015. YouTube video. www.youtube.com/watch?v=37gdL9aZuZA. Accessed May 15, 2021. (video no longer available).

p. 95—Reshma Saujani

Saujani, Reshma. *Girls Who Code: Learn to Code and Change the World.* New York: Viking, 2017, pp. 8–9.

p. 98—Steve Wozniak

Wozniak, Steve and Gina Smith. *iWoz: From Computer Geek to Cult Icon: How I Invented the Personal Computer, Co-Founded Apple, and Had Fun Doing It.* New York: W. W. Norton & Company, 2006, p. 300.

p. 107—Kelvin Doe

Doe, Kelvin. "Moonshot Thinking." Filmed October 10, 2013. Uploaded by Google Israel, November 12, 2013. YouTube video, 9:58. https://www.youtube.com/watch?v=14FBi60V2rg.

p. 114—Fatima Al Kaabi

Al Kaabi, Fatima. "We're all inventors." TEDxFujairah. Uploaded by TEDx Talks, August 29, 2017. YouTube video, 8:02. http://www.youtube.com /watch?v=HrRqah98QYI.

p. 119—Ann Makosinski

Makosinski, Ann. "The Hallow Flashlight." TEDxYouth@Edmonton. Uploaded by TEDx Talks, November 13, 2014. YouTube video, 16:05. https://www.youtube.com/watch?v=VjF2bvYZxkg.

p. 124—Samaira Mehta

Zoom interview. Conducted by Kailei Pew, April 6, 2021.

p. 129—Riya Karumanchi

Karumanchi, Riya. "Taking an Unconventional Path to Unconventional Success." TEDxBrampton. Filmed July 2019. Uploaded by TEDx Talks,

September 9, 2019. YouTube video, 16:20. https://www.youtube.com/watch?v=Qg9B1PXzs10.

p. 135—Yuma Soerianto

Soerianto, Yuma, interviewed by David Lee. "10-year-old app Maker's Plan: Change World, Become Turtle." *BBC News*. June 9, 2017. Video, 1:57. https://www.bbc.com/news/av/technology-40209401.

p. 140—Ehan Kamat

Kamat, Ehan. "In a World of Business Cards, This CEO Brings His Kid Card." TEDxClayton. Uploaded by TEDx Talks, November 22, 2019. YouTube video, 9:23. https://www.youtube.com/watch?v=PIZkL6a2n34.

p. 149—Greta Thunberg

Thunberg, Greta. "Greta Thunberg full speech at UN Climate Change COP24 Conference." COP24 (the 24th Conference of the Parties to the UNFCCC) United Nations Climate Change Summit. Speech given and filmed December 4, 2018. Uploaded by Connect4Climate, December 15, 2018. YouTube video, 3:29. https://www.youtube.com/watch?v=VFkQSGyeCWg.

p. 153—Ken Lou Castillo

Instagram direct message interview. Conducted by Kailei Pew, April 13, 2021.

p. 158—Binish Desai

Johnson, Geoffrey. "Young Inventor of Eco-Friendly Bricks Comes Full Circle." Additional reporting by Andrew Chudzinski. Rotary International website. Originally published in the August 2020 issue of *The Rotarian* magazine. https://www.rotary.org/en/binish-desai-young-inventor-eco-friendly-bricks-comes-full-circle.

p. 166—Deepika Kurup

Kurup, Deepika "Clean Water: A Right or a Privilege?" TEDxNorthHighSchool. Uploaded by TEDx Talks, February 6, 2015. YouTube video, 10:46. https://www.youtube.com/watch?v=b7zLelyelBA.

p. 170—Keiana Cavé

Hauler, Lesley. "Teen Who Created Toxin-Detecting Molecule Wants to Inspire Others in STEM." *Good Morning America*, March 2, 2018.

https://www.goodmorningamerica.com/living/story/teen-created-toxin
-detecting-molecule-inspire-stem-53461050.

p. 177—Asuka Kamiya

Kamiya, Asuka. "How a 12-Year-Old Girl Became One of the Youngest Japanese Patent Holders." Translated by Hiroko Kawano. Interviewed by Kayoko Shiomi. TEDxKyoto. Filmed November 2015. Uploaded by TEDx Talks, December 18, 2015. https://www.youtube.com/watch?v=0nNCXFT_Ots.

p. 182—Gitanjali Rao

Rao, Gitanjali. "Meet TIME's First-Ever Kid of the Year." Interviewed by Angelina Jolie. Transcribed by *Time* staff. *Time* magazine online. December 3, 2020. Video, 3:37. https://time.com/5916772/kid-of-the
-year-2020/.

p. 186—Xóchitl Guadalupe Cruz López

López, Xóchitl Guadalupe Cruz. "Xóchitl Guadalupe Cruz López." Poder Cívico A. C. Uploaded by LaCiudaddelasIdeas. January 11, 2019. YouTube video. https://www.youtube.com/watch?v=_PaOvHgbAoU.

p. 190—Rachel Zimmerman

Email interview. Conducted by Kailei Pew, February 11, 2021.

p. 195—Megan Gambino

Gambino, Megan. "If Necessity Is the Mother of Invention, Then Play Is Its Father." *Smithsonian Magazine*, November 16, 2016. https://www
.smithsonianmag.com/innovation/if-necessity-mother-invention-then
-play-its-father-180961107/.

p. 199—George Epperson

Epperson, George. "My Pop Invented the Popsicle . . . By Accident!" *Reminisce* magazine, July/August 1992: 19. https://i.pinimg.com/originals
/20/61/75/2061750060bc8f8de09b9c774acb7f1e.jpg.

p. 203—George Nissen

De Wyze, Jeannette. "The Man and the Kangaroo." Originally published in the *San Diego Reader*, August 13, 1998. Accessed via Brentwood Trampoline website. https://www.brentwoodtc.org/george_nissen.htm. (Confirmed in an interview with his daughter, Dian Nissen.)

p. 207—Peter Chilvers

Chilvers, Peter. "windsurf from one show." The One Show. Uploaded by bicycleman88, June 10, 2009. YouTube video, 4:11. https://www.youtube.com/watch?v=CQZLKGZ6vgk.

p. 215—Hridayeshwar Singh Bhati

Bhati, Hridayeshwar Singh. "Dhoni Gave Award to Real Life Hero Hridayeshwar Singh Bhati." Edited by Mahesh Jagadappa. Viral Bollywood. Uploaded by Viralbollywood, November 15, 2014. YouTube video, 9:32. https://www.youtube.com/watch?v=_2lFSxCgTmk.

p. 221—Tripp Phillips

Email interview. Conducted by Kailei Pew, January 28, 2021.

p. 228—Jordan Reeves

Reeves, Jordan. *Born Just Right*. New York: Aladdin, 2019, p. 143.

p. 234—Alex Butler

Zoom interview. Conducted by Kailei Pew, April 10, 2021.

p. 236—Adia Bulawa

Email interview. Conducted by Kailei Pew, March 29, 2021.

SELECT SOURCES

Inventions to Solve Daily Problems

Benjamin Franklin

The Franklin Institute. "Benjamin Franklin's Inventions." Benjamin Franklin resources. https://www.fi.edu/benjamin-franklin/inventions. Accessed February 4, 2020.

Franklin, Benjamin. *The Autobiography of Benjamin Franklin.* P F Collier and Son, 1909, pp. 116–117. Google Books, www.google.com/books /edition/The_Autobiography_of_Benjamin_Franklin/Mi0LAAAAIAA.

———. "On the Art of Swimming: In Answer to Some Inquiries of M. Dubourg on the Subject." In *The Works of Dr. Benjamin Franklin; Consisting of Essays, Humorous, Moral, and Literary: With His Life, Written by Himself.* Chiswick, England: the Press of C. Whittingham, College House, 1824. pp. 191–193. Google Books, https://books.google.com/books?id=TIgTAAAAQAAJ.

Benjamin Franklin House. "Live Science Class for Kids: Ben Franklin's Swim Fins." Events. https://benjaminfranklinhouse.org/event/virtual -class-ben-franklins-swim-fins/. Accessed February 10, 2020.

The Franklin Institute. "Youth and Community Programs." https:// www.fi.edu/youth-community-programs. Accessed February 10, 2020.

Louis Braille

Braille, Louis. *Procedure for Writing Words, Music and Plain-Song Using Dots for the Use of the Blind and Made Available to Them by L. Braille, Instructor at the Royal Institution of Blind Youth.* 1829. Translated by the National Federation of the Blind, https://nfb.org /images/nfb/publications/braille/thefirstpublicationofthebraillecode englishtranslation.html.

Freedman, Russell. *Out of Darkness: The Story of Louis Braille.* New York: Clarion Books, 1997.

Frith, Margaret. *Who Was Louis Braille?* New York: Penguin Workshop, 2014.

BBC Ideas. "The Incredible Story of the Boy Who Invented Braille." June 22, 2019. YouTube video, 3:30. http://www.youtube.com/watch?v =o9BOQ6IpTSE.

Keller, Helen. "Braille, the Magic Wand of the Blind." Typewritten essay (unpublished),1929. Accessed via the American Foundation for the Blind website. Accessed May 12, 2021. https://www.afb.org/about-afb/history /helen-keller/books-essays-speeches/education/braille-magic-wand-blind.

Kushner, Sherrill. "The Story of Louis Braille." Paths to Literacy, January 2005. https://www.pathstoliteracy.org/story-louis-braille.

Library of Congress "Louis Braille: His Legacy and Influence." Exhibitions. November 5, 2009–January 30, 2010. https://www.loc.gov/exhibits/louis -braille/.

Mellor, C. Michael. *Louis Braille: A Touch of Genius*. Boston: National Braille Press, 2006.

Stein, Deborah Kent. "Louis Braille: The Father of Literacy for the Blind." *The National Federation of the Blind Magazine for Parents and Teachers of Blind Children, Special Issue: A Celebration of Braille* 28, no. 1 (2009). Accessed via the National Federation of the Blind. Accessed July 1, 2021. https://nfb .org//sites/default/files/images/nfb/publications/fr/fr28/fr280105.htm.

Kathryn "KK" Gregory

Polartec. "Fabrics." Fabrics. https://www.polartec.com/fabrics.

Gregory, Kathryn. "About KK Gregory, Inventor of Wristies®" Wristies. https://www.wristies.com/KK_Wristies_Inventor_s/152.htm. Accessed January 25, 2021.

———. "A Note From KK, Owner, MillYardage LLC." About Us. Mill Yardage. https://www.millyardage.com/aboutus.asp. Accessed August 9, 2021.

Gregory, Kathryn, and Susan B. Gregory. Article of thermal clothing for covering the underlying area at the gap between a coat sleeve and a glove. US Patent US5864886A, filed June 24, 1996, and issued February 2, 1999. https://patents.google.com/patent/US5864886.

"K-K Gregory: Wristies®." Massachusetts Institute of Technology. https:// lemelson.mit.edu/resources/k-k-gregory. Accessed January 25, 2021.

Wristies. "Wristies, Inc—The Company." Company Info. https://www.wristies .com/aboutus.asp. Accessed January 25, 2021.

Richie Stachowski

Knight Ridder Newspapers. "Boy Inventor Readying Splash in Toy Market." *Chicago Tribune*. February 15, 1998. https://www.chicagotribune.com /news/ct-xpm-1998-02-15-9802150459-story.html.

Science Buddies and Sabine De Brabandere. "What Do You Hear Underwater?" Bring Science Home. *Scientific American*. June 27, 2019. https://www.scientificamerican.com/article/what-do-you-hear-underwater/.

National Oceanic and Atmospheric Administration. "How Far Does Sound Travel in the Ocean?" National Ocean Service. Last modified January 20, 2023. https://oceanservice.noaa.gov/facts/sound.html.

"Richie Stachowski: Water Talkies™." Massachusetts Institute of Technology. https://lemelson.mit.edu/resources/richie-stachowski. Accessed January 27, 2021.

National Museum of Education. "Richie Stachowski." National Gallery for America's Young Inventors - 1997 Keynote Speaker. https://www.nmoe.org/individual/richie-stachowski.

Stachowski, Richie C. Device for talking underwater. US Patent US5877460A, filed September 16, 1997, and issued March 2, 1999. https://patents.google.com/patent/US5877460A/en.

Karoli Hindriks

Hindriks, Karoli. "Borders Are Within Us." TEDxAmsterdamWomen. Uploaded by TEDx Talks, November 16, 2017. YouTube video, 10:16. https://www.youtube.com/watch?v=-cTOfeIlz1I.

WEgate. "From Reflective Clothing to Recruitment: Estonian Entrepreneur's Dream to 'Make a Difference in the World.'" WEgate: European Gateway for Women's Entrepreneurship. Last updated January 30, 2023. https://www.wegate.eu/project-items/from-reflective-clothing-to-recruitment-estonian-entrepreneurs-dream-to-make-a-difference-in-the-world/.

Hindriks, Karoli. Email interview. Conducted by Kailei Pew, January 18, 2022.

JAEuropeAdmin. "How Entrepreneurial Education Changed the Life of Karoli Hindriks, Founder and CEO of Jobbatical." Switch On Europe. European Entrepreneurship Education NETwork. April 24, 2017. https://switchoneurope.org/how-entrepreneurial-education-changed-the-life-of-karoli-hindriks-founder-and-ceo-of-jobbatical/.

Littman, Jonathan and Susanna Camp. "The Guardian: Karoli Hindriks." SmartUp: The Innovation Hub. September 7, 2020. https://smartup.life/the-guardian-karoli-hindriks/.

Tamkivi, Ede Schank. "Standing Out from the Crowd: Karoli Hindriks. Founder

of Jobbatical." *Estonian World*, September 15, 2016. https://estonian
world.com/people/standing-crowd-karoli-hindriks-founder-jobbatical/.

Cassidy Goldstein

By Kids For Kids. "BKFK Media." Uploaded by IdeaLocker, January 22, 2010.
YouTube video, 4:25. https://www.youtube.com/watch?v=kz9kzDaw57w.

"Cassidy Is Named Inventor of the Year." Intellectual Property Organization Inventor of the Year 2006. Uploaded by IdeaLocker, September 29,
2009. https://www.youtube.com/watch?v=6BYzGMyRzus.

"Cassidy Goldstein: Crayon Holder." Massachusetts Institute of Technology.
https://lemelson.mit.edu/resources/cassidy-goldstein. Accessed April
16, 2021.

CNN. "Innovators: Norm Goldstein, BKFK." Uploaded by IdeaLocker, November 12, 2010. YouTube video, 3:35. https://www.youtube.com/watch?
v=UATIt6E1fFE.

Goldstein, Cassidy. Device for holding a writing instrument. US Patent
US6402407B1, filed June 29, 2000, and issued June 11, 2002. https://
patents.google.com/patent/US6402407B1/en.

Goldstein, Norm. "Norm Goldstein Speaks at Congressional Caucus." By
Kids For Kids. Uploaded by IdeaLocker, February 17, 2012. YouTube
video, 5:33. https://www.youtube.com/watch?v=4sWWXu92mjg.

———. Zoom interview. Conducted by Kailei Pew, April 19, 2021.

———. "Inventive Thinking Toolkit." The By Kids for Kids Xerox Inventive
Thinking Toolkit Program. Uploaded by IdeaLocker, June 19, 2009. YouTube
video, 9:21. https://www.youtube.com/watch?v=NYR2uWefulk.

Sofia Overton

KUAF National Public Radio. "Bentonville Teen to Appear on 'Shark Tank.'"
Interview by Antoinette Grajeda. Ozarks at Large. January 9, 2020.
https://www.kuaf.com/post/bentonville-teen-appear-shark-tank.

Heyn, Beth. "WisePocket Products on 'Shark Tank': 5 Fast Facts You Need to
Know." Heavy Inc. August 21, 2020. https://heavy.com/entertainment
/2020/01/wisepocket-products-shark-tank/ Accessed July 26, 2021. (no
longer available).

Lee, Tiffany. "Bentonville 14-Year-Old Business Owner Makes Deal on Shark
Tank." KFSM Digital. January 17, 2020. www.thv11.com/article/money

/business/bentonville-14-year-old-business-owner-makes-deal-on-shark
-tank/91-208c6766-1c7c-4c02-a894-2bea3234db47.

Locke, Taylor. "This 13-year-old Saved $10,000 to Start a 'Socks with Pock-
ets' Business—and Got a 5-figure Deal on 'Shark Tank.'" CNBC online. Success: Startups. Updated January 13, 2020. https://www.cnbc
.com/2020/01/13/shark-tank-teen-saved-thousands-for-socks-with
-pockets-business.html.

WisePocket Products. "Our Story." About us. https://wisepocketproducts
.com/pages/about-us Accessed December 2022. (site discontinued).

Overton, Sofia. Double cuff pocket sock. US Patent USD871052S1, filed
January 18, 2018, and issued December 31, 2019. https://patents.google
.com/patent/USD871052S1.

Overton, Sofia. "WisePocket Products." Indiegogo. https://www.indiegogo
.com/projects/wise-pocket-products#/.

Overton, Sofie. "WisePocket Indiegogo v2." January 18, 2018. YouTube video,
3:28. https://www.youtube.com/watch?v=7BdrD9g_Ow0.

Inventions to Help Others

Spencer Whale

Casey, Susan. *Kids Inventing! A Handbook for Young Inventors*. Hoboken,
NJ: Jossey-Bass, 2005.

Chapid, Sandra. "Spencer y Brandon Whale." Momento Infantil. Uploaded
by Sandra Chapid, September 17, 2020. YouTube video, 3:19. https://
www.youtube.com/watch?v=fdu8aYautiI.

National Museum of Education. "Spencer Rocco Whale." KidKare Hospital
Equipment & Supplies. Accessed April 5, 2021. https://www.nmoe.org
/individual/spencer-rocco-whale.

Day, Fran, RN and the PCH IV Team. "IVs." The Emily Center at the Phoenix Children's Hospital. https://www.phoenixchildrens.org/files/inline
-files/IVs-107.pdf. Accessed April 5, 2021.

Luton, L. Grant. "Spencer Rocco Whale." Illustrated by Ryan Humbert.
The Partnership for America's Future. National Museum of Education. 2000. https://www.nmoe.org/sites/default/files/2021-01/00
_whale2.jpg.

Wolf, Theo. "Coach Profiles: Introducing Spencer Whale." Spike Lab, May 7, 2020. https://spikelab.com/coach-profiles-introducing-spencer -whale/.

Whale, Spencer R. Toy vehicle adapted for medical use. US Patent US20050161933A1, filed January 6, 2005, and issued July 28, 2005. https://patents.google.com/patent/US20050161933A1/en.

Remya Jose

BrightVibes. "14-Year-Old Indian Schoolgirl Invents a Pedal-Powered Washing Machine." Uploaded by BrightVibes, March 2, 2018. YouTube video, 2:23. https://www.youtube.com/watch?v=J5QlwG-mJRk.

Agarwal, Ayushi. "Remya Jose Creates Washing Machine Which Runs Without Electricity." Indian Women Blog. October 13, 2015. https:// www.indianwomenblog.org/remya-jose-creates-washing-machine -which-runs-without-electricity/.

James, T. J. "Washing Cum Exercise Machine." National Innovation Foundation of India. https://nif.org.in/upload/innovation/3rd/312-washing -cum-exercise-machine.pdf.

Jose, Remya. A Manual Washing Machine. Indian Patent 207634, filed August 7, 2003, and issued. November 2, 2007. https://www.allindianpatents .com/patents/207634-a-manual-washing-machine.

Associated Press. "Pedal Powered Washing Machine Takes the Hard Work Out of Laundry." Uploaded by AP Archive, July 23, 2015. YouTube video, 4:25. https://www.youtube.com/watch?v=93en7nhKUSM.

NDTV. "Remya Jose's Pedal Washing Machine." Uploaded by rahulbrown, May 23, 2008. YouTube video, 5:53. https://www.youtube.com/watch?v =VhlUVdbU9Lk.

Lily Born

Born, Joe. "Kangaroo Cups: A Better Anti-Spill Cup." Kickstarter. November 11, 2016. https://www.kickstarter.com/projects/joeborn/kangaroo-cups -plastic.

Chudik, Ella. "July Inventor Spotlight: Lily Born." Spark Shop. July 2019. https://www.sparkshop.org/news-and-events/2019/8/8/july-inventor -spotlight-lily-born.

"CNN Heroes Young Wonder: Lily Born." CNN, February 26, 2015. Video, 1:53.

https://www.cnn.com/videos/tv/2015/02/26/cnnheroes-young-wonder
-lily-born.cnn.

Born, Lily. "Kangaroo Cup Kickstarter Video 2014." Uploaded by Joe Born, June 18, 2014. YouTube video, 2:34. https://www.youtube.com/watch? v=bKhrEH0rhcg.

Bootstrapping in America. Speakers Lily and Joe Born. "Lily Born of Kangaroo Cup, Bootstrapping in America." Uploaded by tastytrade, December 18, 2014. YouTube video. https://www.youtube.com/watch?v= gOrPjjBBGBA. Accessed June 4, 2021. (no longer available).

Born, Lily. "Lily Telling the Kangaroo Cup Story at Teen Ignite." Naperville Teen Ignite. Uploaded by Joe Born, June 21, 2014. YouTube video, 5:37. https://www.youtube.com/watch?v=JmvjTJP3-Rw.

Moss, Caroline. "Brilliant 11-Year-Old Designs an Unbreakable, Spill-Proof Cup for Her Ailing Grandpa." *Business Insider*, June 6, 2014. https:// www.businessinsider.com/unbreakable-kangaroo-cups-2014-6.

Born, Joe. "The Original Kangaroo Cup Story." October 11, 2012. YouTube video, 3:34. https://www.youtube.com/watch?v=TdyJKo0eHhk.

Born, Lily. "Update from Lily on the Kangaroo Cups." Uploaded by Joe Born, September 29, 2013. YouTube video, 2:09. https://www.youtube .com/watch?v=ANooknssNGg.

Bishop Curry V

Brown, Maressa. "This Brilliant 11-Year-Old Received a Patent on His Invention to Prevent Hot Car Deaths." *Parents Magazine*, August 27, 2018. http://www.parents.com/kids/this-brilliant-11-year-old-received -a-patent-on-his-invention-to-prevent-hot-car-deaths/. Accessed July 22, 2022. (no longer available).

Curry, Bishop, V. Zoom interview. Conducted by Kailei Pew, March 10, 2021.

Dahlgren, Kristen, and Daniel Arkin. "11-Year-Old Texas Boy Invents Device to Prevent Hot Car Deaths." NBC News. Last updated June 29, 2017. https://www.nbcnews.com/storyline/hot-cars-and-kids/11-year-old -texas-boy-invents-device-prevent-hot-car-n777876.

Fulling, Janie. "11-Year-Old's Invention Could Prevent Hot Car Deaths." *USA Today*. Last updated July 18, 2017. https://www.usatoday.com/story /news/humankind/2017/07/18/11-year-olds-invention-could-prevent -hot-car-deaths/476057001/.

Curry, Bishop. "I Don't Think Babies Should Die in Hot Cars." TEDxPlano. Uploaded by TEDx Talks, April 18, 2018. YouTube video, 9:09. https://www.youtube.com/watch?v=l1XKRpBRZJA.

Oasis. "Oasis Marketing Video." Silver Moon Company. Uploaded by Tia Curry, March 10, 2021. YouTube video, 2.24. https://www.youtube.com/watch?v=h6j61BW8wK8.

Cassidy Crowley

Baby Toon, The. "The Baby Toon Transformation." February 28, 2020. YouTube video, 0:18. https://www.youtube.com/watch?v=hVheTyTjD4g.

Crowley, Cassidy. "Cassidy Crowley Talks About Inventing the Baby Toon." Uploaded by The Baby Toon, February 28, 2020. YouTube video, 1:10. https://www.youtube.com/watch?v=8RO70HUkNcA.

Brier, Sherry. "Cassidy Crowley – 10 Year-Old Inventor." Women Rock Project. https://womenrockproject.com/cassidy-crowley-10-year-old-inventor/.

Crowley, Cassidy, and Lori Crowley. Feeding spoon. US Patent: USD823073S1, filed August 1, 2017, and issued July 17, 2018. https://patents.google.com/patent/USD823073S1/.

Murphy, Ellie and Ali Murphy. "How the Baby Toon Landed a Deal on Shark Tank—With Its Founder and Developer." October 30, 2019. Hawaii's Best Travel. Podcast. MP3 audio, 10:13. https://www.hawaiisbesttravel.com/episode017/.

Kobayashi, Collin. Email interview, Conducted by Kailei Pew, April 13, 2021.

Monton, Nicole. "Baby Shark." *Hawaii Island Midweek*. January 6, 2021. https://www.hawaiiislandmidweek.com/cassidy-crowley-the-baby-toon/.

Shark Tank. "Ten-Year-Old Cassidy Crowley Gets a Deal and Gets to Sit in a Shark Chair." Uploaded by ABC, September 29, 2019. YouTube video, 3:04. https://www.youtube.com/watch?v=Gb3UKbSS48g.

Baby Toon website, The. https://thebabytoon.com/.

Baby Toon, The. Facebook, https://www.facebook.com/thebabytoon/.

3D Innovations. "The Baby Toon." November 27, 2017. https://www.3d-innovations.com/blog/portfolio/babytoon/.

Dasia Taylor

PBS NewsHour. "17-Year-Old Makes Color Changing Sutures that Detect Infection." July 22, 2021. YouTube video, 6:25. https://www.youtube.com/watch?v=DMeH0Hhs14c.

Dunlap, Natalie. "Black History Game Show Club Prepares for Des Moines Competition." *West Side Story: The Student News Source of Iowa City West High*. January 22, 2020. https://wsspaper.com/55854/news/black-history-game-show-club-prepares-for-des-moines-competition/#photo.

Machemer, Theresa. "This High Schooler Invented Color-Changing Sutures to Detect Infection." *Smithsonian Magazine*, March 25, 2021. https://www.smithsonianmag.com/innovation/high-schooler-invented-color-changing-sutures-detect-infection-180977345/.

Cosgrove, Miranda. "Meet the Teenage Scientist Who Invented Color Changing Sutures." Uploaded by Mission Unstoppable, August 11, 2021. YouTube video, 4:59. https://www.youtube.com/watch?v=-gfuL_QsFfk.

USA Science & Engineering Festival. "Next Gen STEM Student Researchers and Innovators- Dasia Taylor and Catherine Kim." xSTEM All Access Free Interactive Speaker Series. May 11, 2022. https://www.youtube.com/watch?v=0VQSkwXVG5Q.

Taylor, Dasia. "Regeneron STS 2021-Dasia Taylor." Uploaded by Societyfor-Science, March 31, 2021. https://www.youtube.com/watch?v=0y0TOU1pe40.

Spencer, Christian. "Black Teen, Dasia Taylor, Is the Inventor of a Method to Detect Surgical Infections." *Black Enterprise*, March 30, 2021. https://www.blackenterprise.com/black-teen-dasia-taylor-is-the-inventor-of-a-method-to-detect-surgical-infections/.

Inventions in Technology

Steve Wozniak

Woz.org. "About Steve Wozniak aka 'The Woz.'" Steve Wozniak. About. http://www.woz.org/about/.

Wozniak, Steve. "An Evening with Steve Wozniak." Uploaded by Computer History Museum, December 7, 2007. YouTube video, 1:30:56. https://www.youtube.com/watch?v=rJ8IgX8RikM.

Levy, Steven. "The Brief History of the ENIAC Computer." *Smithsonian Magazine*. November 2013. https://www.smithsonianmag.com/history/the-brief-history-of-the-eniac-computer-3889120/.

Mitchell-Whittington, Michelle. "Childhood Chat Shaped Steve Wozniak, Apple and the Computer Revolution." *Brisbane Times*. Updated August 28, 2016. https://www.brisbanetimes.com.au/national/queensland /childhood-chat-shaped-steve-wozniak-apple-and-the-computer-revo lution-20160826-gr2bpk.html.

The Henry Ford Museum of American Innovation. "On Innovation: Steve Wozniak." April 29, 2010. YouTube video, 6:44. https://www.youtube .com/watch?v=Nn_N0dOMbYM.

Wozniak, Steve. "How Steve Wozniak Became the Genius Who Invented the Personal Computer." Gizmodo. July 17, 2012. https://gizmodo.com/how -steve-wozniak-became-the-genius-who-invented-the-pe-5926688.

Wozniak, Steve, and Gina Smith. *iWoz: From Computer Geek to Cult Icon: How I Invented the Personal Computer, Co-Founded Apple, and Had Fun Doing It*. New York: W. W. Norton & Company, 2006.

Kelvin Doe
THINKR: Prodigies. "15-Yr-Old Kelvin Doe Wows M.I.T." Created and produced by RadicalMedia. Uploaded by THNKR, November 16, 2012. YouTube video, 10:06. https://www.youtube.com/watch?v=XOLOLrUBRBY.

Doe, Kelvin. "Changing Africa's Narrative." TEDxLusaka. Uploaded by TEDx Talks, October 12, 2016. YouTube video, 14:08. https://www.youtube .com/watch?v=KLgpyNhYSTo.

Mocomi. "How Do Batteries Work?" Mocomi & Anibrain Digital Technologies. Uploaded by MocomiKids, July 3, 2013. YouTube video, 2:14. https://www.youtube.com/watch?v=gWKOjncBMCQ.

Make Magazine. "Meet Young Makers Panel Discussion on Make: Live Stage at World Maker Faire." Moderated by Mark Greenlaw. September 30, 2012. YouTube video, 48:05. https://www.youtube.com/watch?v=uidBev5rNqQ.

Doe, Kelvin. "Persistent Experimentation." TEDxTeen. Uploaded by TEDx Talks, March 23, 2013. YouTube video, 12:22. https://www.youtube .com/watch?v=wQigsI3xsHw.

THINKR: Prodigies. "Prodigy from Sierra Leone Builds Battery." Created and produced by RadicalMedia. Uploaded by THNKR, November 20, 2012. YouTube video, 1:42. https://www.youtube.com/watch?v=B86lhnHyFCw.

Roach, John. "Whiz Kid from Sierra Leone Built Own Battery, Radio, Transmitter." NBC News. November 20, 2012. https://www.nbcnews.com/tech

/tech-news/whiz-kid-sierra-leone-built-own-battery-radio-transmitter
-flna1c7179394.

Sengeh, David. "DIY Africa: Empowering a New Sierra Leone." CNN, November 14, 2012. https://web.archive.org/web/20121120055204/http://whatsnext .blogs.cnn.com/2012/11/14/diy-africa-empowering-a-new-sierra-leone/.

Fatima Al Kaabi

Al Kaabi, Fatima. Email interview. Conducted by Kailei Pew, July 28, 2020; August 11, 2020; January 23, 2021; and February 2, 2021.

Ericsson MEA "Ericsson Catches Up with Fatima Al Kaabi, UAE's Youngest Emirati Inventor." Uploaded by Ericsson MEA, June 14, 2021. https:// www.youtube.com/watch?v=8tz10Rf-MtQ. Accessed February 27, 2022. (no longer available).

Mohamed, Hatem. "Mohamed bin Zayed Receives UAE's Youngest Inventor Fatima Al Kaabi." WAM - Emirates News Agency. December 15, 2017. https://www.wam.ae/en/details/1395302656499.

Pupic, Tamara. "She Was Once Declared the UAE's Youngest Inventor— And Now, Fatima Al Kaabi Wants to Help Other Girls Follow Her Lead." *Entrepreneur Middle East*. June 21, 2021. https://www.entrepreneur .com/article/375106.

Sagar, Sangeetha. "Meet the UAE's Youngest Inventor." *Friday Magazine*. August 27, 2020. https://gulfnews.com/friday/art-people/meet-the-uaes -youngest-inventor-1.2309189.

Thomas, Tess. "18-year-old Inventor Fatima Alkaabi on Why the World Needs Girls to Study AI." Assembly: A Malala Fund Publication. March 4, 2020. https://assembly.malala.org/stories/fatima-alkaabi-on-girls-and -articial-intelligence.

Al Kaabi, Fatima. "We're all inventors." TEDxFujairah. Uploaded by TEDx Talks, August 29, 2017. YouTube video, 8:02. http://www.youtube.com /watch?v=HrRqah98QYI.

Ann Makosinski

Beilstein, Saul. "Girl Invents 'Hollow' Flashlight." Shaw TV Victoria. Up- loaded by ShawTVSouthVI, July 10, 2013. YouTube video, 3:42. https:// www.youtube.com/watch?v=DLECJbWrKrs.

Makosinski, Ann. "Inventing the Hollow Flashlight and the Future of En- ergy Saving Technology." USA Science & Engineering Festival. xSTEM

2016, Washington, DC. Uploaded by USA Science & Engineering Festival, October 3, 2017. YouTube video, 21:03. https://www.youtube.com/watch?v=V_7VkL0CUB4.

Makosinski, Ann, and Arthur Makosinski. Thermoelectrically powered portable light source. US Patent US10178713B2, filed June 26, 2017, and issued January 8, 2019. https://patents.google.com/patent/US10178713B2/.

Nguyen, Tuan C. "This Flashlight Is Powered by the Touch of Your Hand." *Smithsonian Magazine*. March 24, 2014. https://www.smithsonianmag.com/innovation/this-flashlight-is-powered-by-the-touch-of-your-hand-180950226/.

NBC News. "Teen Inventor's Bright Idea May Light Up the World." May 12, 2014. https://www.nbcnews.com/nightly-news/teen-inventors-bright-idea-may-light-world-n103601.

Makosinski, Ann. "The Hallow Flashlight." TEDxYouth@Edmonton. Uploaded by TEDx Talks, November 13, 2014. YouTube video, 16:05. https://www.youtube.com/watch?v=VjF2bvYZxkg.

Makosinski, Ann. "The Hollow (Thermoelectric) Flashlight-Google Science Fair." Uploaded by Andini, May 1, 2013. YouTube video, 2:05. https://www.youtube.com/watch?v=9CCGUMkcbjg.

Samaira Mehta

Career Girls. "10-Year-Old Founder and CEO." Uploaded by careergirls, August 8, 2019. https://www.youtube.com/watch?v=KfSa8SQXyIw.

Mehta, Samaira. "My Mission." CoderBunnyz website. Main page. https://www.coderbunnyz.com/.

CNBC Make It. "Meet The 10-Year-Old Coder Grabbing Google's Attention." April 29, 2019. YouTube video, 4:55. https://www.youtube.com/watch?v=UKksIo79Jbc.

Mehta, Samaira. Zoom interview. Conducted by Kailei Pew, April 6, 2021.

Yes, One Billion Kids Can Code. "Our Mission." About page. https://www.yesonebillionkidscancode.org/about.

Rich, Gina. "Samaira Mehta Shows Other Kids the Fun of Coding by Inventing Board Games." *The Washington Post*. February 9, 2021. https://www.washingtonpost.com/lifestyle/kidspost/early-on-samaira-mehta-learned-coding-is-fun-now-shes-spreading-the-word/2021/02/08/093ce42e-6000-11eb-9061-07abcc1f9229_story.html.

Creator University Series "The 12-Year-Old CEO of the World's First AI Board Game." Uploaded by First Code Academy, March 2, 2021. YouTube video, 28:13. https://www.youtube.com/watch?v=AIHEhBlwrN4.

Riya Karumanchi

Boisvert, Nick. "How a 15-Year-Old Entrepreneur Is Reinventing the Standard White Cane with Smart Technology." CBC News, Toronto. September 1, 2018. https://www.cbc.ca/news/canada/toronto/smart-cane -company-1.4806713.

"The Global Positioning System." The National Coordination Office for Space-Based Positioning, Navigation, and Timing. Last modified February 22, 2021. https://www.gps.gov/systems/gps/.

AMI: Accessible Media Inc. "Introducing the SmartCane in Toronto." November 20, 2018. YouTube video, 5:22. https://www.youtube.com/watch?v =NIn-daIS_oc.

Karumanchi, Riya. "Riya Karumanchi on TKS & Founding Smartcane." Uploaded by The FLIK Team, August 1, 2020. YouTube video, 5:46. https://www.youtube.com/watch?v=YGqHKHYhGDo.

Maw, Isaac. "Grade 9 Science Fair Wunderkind Creates a Smarter White Cane." Engineering. February 4, 2018. https://www.engineering .com/story/grade-9-science-fair-wunderkind-creates-a-smarter-white -cane.

Reilly, Emma. "Burlington Teen Is an Entrepreneur, an Inventor and Hopes to 'Be the Change.'" *Toronto News*. August 28, 2017. https://www.thespec .com/news/hamilton-region/2017/08/28/burlington-teen-is-an-entre preneur-an-inventor-and-hopes-to-be-the-change.html.

Karumanchi, Riya. "Riya Karumanchi." LinkedIn. https://www.linkedin.com /in/riya-karumanchi/.

Karumanchi, Riya. "Taking an Unconventional Path to Unconventional Success." TEDxBrampton. Filmed July 2019. Uploaded by TEDx Talks, September 9, 2019. YouTube video, 16:20. https://www.youtube.com /watch?v=Qg9B1PXzs10.

Karumanchi, Riya. "Welcome to the Next 100 Years of Our Lives." TEDx-McMasterU. Filmed December 2019. Uploaded by TEDx Talks, February 3, 2020. YouTube video, 14:14. https://www.youtube.com/watch?v=UzP KgDmOqsg.

Yuma Soerianto

Apple Inc. "Meet the Developer: Yuma Soerianto." Apple. App Store Preview. https://apps.apple.com/au/story/id1382397261.

Soerianto, Yuma. "Apple WWDC17 Scholarship submission {Accepted}." Uploaded by Anyone Can Code, May 6, 2017. YouTube video, 2:53. https://www.youtube.com/watch?v=zkUZ2D9sSqo.

Cook, Tim. "Apple—WWDC 2017 Keynote." Apple Worldwide Developers Conference 2017 Keynote Address. Filmed June 5, 2017 at the San Jose Convention Center, San Jose, CA. Uploaded by Apple, June 9, 2017. https://www.youtube.com/watch?v=oaqHdULqet0.

Graham, Jefferson. "10-Year-Old App Developer's Advice to Other Kids: Get Coding Now." *USA Today*. June 8, 2017. https://www.usatoday.com/story/tech/talkingtech/2017/06/08/10-year-old-app-developers-advice-other-kids-get-coding-now/102587614/.

Soerianto, Yuma, interviewed by David Lee. "10-year-old app Maker's Plan: Change World, Become Turtle." *BBC News*. June 9, 2017. Video, 1:57. https://www.bbc.com/news/av/technology-40209401.

AR Critic. "Let's Stack AR!—Developed by a 10-Year-Old Developer Yuma Soerianto." November 19, 2017. YouTube video, 5:16. https://www.youtube.com/watch?v=ggAqGMZ0LLY.

Soerianto, Yuma. "My Highlights." Made By Yuma. https://www.madebyyuma.com/highlights/index.html.

Soerianto, Yuma. "Youngest WWDC Scholarship Winner for 4 Years Webinar." Webinar. Uploaded by Hour of Code Hong Kong, July 23, 2020. YouTube video, 38:37. https://www.youtube.com/watch?v=I9tYNwlDvPk.

Inventions for the Environment

Ken Lou Castillo

Castillo, Ken Lou. Instagram direct message interview. Conducted by Kailei Pew, April 13, 2021.

Castillo, Ken Lou. "La Chispa Chapina Con Ken Lou." Produced by Esther Garcia, USAC TV: La Television Alternativa. 2017. Uploaded by albertolou, April 19, 2017. YouTube video, 9:51. https://www.youtube.com/watch?v=XH714YkdvhA.

Harding, Scharon. "Latin America News: Guatemalan Who Invented Eco-Friendly Mr. Fuego Firewood at Age 9 Laments Country's Increasing

Deforestation Rates." *Latin Post*. July 16, 2014. https://www.latinpost
.com/articles/17359/20140716/latin-america-news-guatemalan-who
-invented-eco-friendly-mr-fuego.htm.

Martínez, Saúl. "El Inventor Más Joven de Guatemala se Centra en la Defen-
sa del Medioambiente." EFE:Verde. July 14, 2014. https://www.efeverde
.com/noticias/el-inventor-mas-joven-de-guatemala-se-centra-en-la
-defensa-del-medioambiente.

Castillo, Ken Lou. "Mr Fuego—by Ken Lou (made in Guatemala)." Produced
by Fusion. Uploaded by Gua 14–90, March 23, 2017. YouTube video, 2:03.
https://www.youtube.com/watch?v=HIkwfPRgvmw.

"Mr. Fuego: Instant Flame." Mr. Fuego. https://www.mrfuego.com/.

Castillo, Ken Lou. "Mr Fuego Project Earth." The Seekers. Project Earth.
Produced by Fusion. Uploaded by albertolou, March 23, 2017. https://
www.youtube.com/watch?v=Euq5CfEEHXc.

Binish Desai

Balaji, Roshni. "This 26-Year-Old Is Making Value Out of Waste and Paving
Way for a Greener Environment." Social Story, May 17, 2020. https://
yourstory.com/socialstory/2020/05/binish-desai-recycling-waste-products
-environment/amp.

Rotary International. "Binish Desai, Inventor of Eco-Friendly Bricks,
Comes Full Circle." Uploaded by Rotary. April 14, 2021. YouTube video,
1:39. https://www.youtube.com/watch?v=tlwvVzXcnpk.

Chandwani, Nikhil. *The Recycle Man: Story of Dr. Binish Desai's Life and
Works*. India: Raindrop Publishers, 2019.

Desai, Binish. Eco Eclectic Tech website. https://www.binishdesai.com/.

Dutta, Taniya. "The Pandemic Is Generating Tons of Discarded PPE. This
Entrepreneur Is Turning It into Bricks." *The Washington Post*, December 23, 2020. https://www.washingtonpost.com/road-to-recovery
/covid-ppe-waste-recycling-india/2020/11/24/298a5c12-285f-11eb-9c21
-3cc501d0981f_story.html.

Johnson, Geoffrey. "Young Inventor of Eco-Friendly Bricks Comes Full Circle." Additional reporting by Andrew Chudzinski. Rotary International
website. Originally published in the August 2020 issue of *The Rotarian* magazine. https://www.rotary.org/en/binish-desai-young-inventor
-eco-friendly-bricks-comes-full-circle.

Desai, Binesh. "Meet Binish Desai!" CNBC TV Channel 18 India. Uploaded by CNBC-TV18, September 11, 2020. YouTube video, 1:54. https://www.youtube.com/watch?v=YNduR9w-B24.

Desai, Binish. "Waste into Eco Treasure by the Recycle Man of India." TEDxSayajigunj, June 2018. Video, 9:16. https://www.ted.com/talks/binish_desai_waste_into_eco_treasure_by_the_recycle_man_of_india.

Deepika Kurup

Kurup, Deepika. "A Young Scientist's Quest for Clean Water." TED Talks. Filmed in San Francisco, CA, October 2016. Uploaded by TED, February 17, 2017. YouTube video, 7:59. https://www.youtube.com/watch?v=AkUcaludrcI.

Kurup, Deepika "Clean Water: A Right or a Privilege?" TEDxNorthHighSchool. Uploaded by TEDx Talks, February 6, 2015. YouTube video, 10:46. https://www.youtube.com/watch?v=b7zLeIyeIBA.

"Deepika Kurup Wants to Save the World Through Clean Water." *Brown Girl Magazine*, May 1, 2013, www.browngirlmagazine.com/2013/05/brown-girl-of-the-month-deepika-kurup-wants-to-save-world-through-clean-water/.

Kurup, Deepika. "Global Solutions, a Drop at a Time." TEDxAmoskeag Millyard. Filmed in 2014. Uploaded by TEDx Talks, June 15, 2015. https://www.youtube.com/watch?v=h4Cz41mKfYs.

Kurup, Deepika. "Novel Photocatalytic Pervious Composites for Removing Multiple Classes of Toxins from Water." Filmed for the Davidson Fellow Scholarship. Uploaded by Deepika Kurup, July 16, 2015. YouTube video, 9:42. https://www.youtube.com/watch?v=NEDRL4igPaA.

Ramaswamy, Jothi. "Deepika Kurup Interview." ThinkSTEAM. October 28, 2015. https://www.thinksteam4girls.org/deepika-kurup-interview/.

Keiana Cavé

Cavé, Keiana. "A Method for Identifying the Photoproducts, Mechanisms, and Toxicity of Petroleum from the Deepwater Horizon by High-Performance Liquid Chromatography and DNPHi Derivatization." Submitted Manuscript. Science AAAS. Accessed via www.academia.edu/15692861.

Hauler, Lesley. "Teen Who Created Toxin-Detecting Molecule Wants to Inspire Others in STEM." *Good Morning America*, March 2, 2018. https://www.goodmorningamerica.com/living/story/teen-created-toxin-detecting-molecule-inspire-stem-53461050.

Cavé, Keiana. "Keiana Cave Presenting at PLTW Summit 2017." PLTW Summit 2017. Uploaded by Project Lead the Way, February 9, 2018. YouTube video, 6:11. https://www.youtube.com/watch?v=ZnT_tbhmp_w.

Kolcon, Margaret. "Student of the Year: Keiana Cavé." *Michigan Daily*. April 11, 2017. https://www.michigandaily.com/statement/student-of-the-year-keiana-cave/.

Seymour, Allison. "The Color of STEM Ep#1 Keiana Cavé." The Color of STEM, January 31, 2016. YouTube video, 4:51. https://www.youtube.com/watch?v=FKRmRYl3qwg.

Cavé, Keiana. "The Art of Goal Setting." TEDxUofM. Uploaded by TEDx Talks, March 13, 2018. YouTube video, 14:57. https://www.youtube.com/watch?v=9LYG5Tx-aWs.

Cavé, Keiana. "The Power of Being Obnoxious." TEDxESADE. Uploaded by TEDx Talks, June 19, 2017. YouTube video, 14:03. https://www.youtube.com/watch?v=Y5mRHsm2g4g.

Asuka Kamiya

Grape Japan Editorial Staff. "This 12-Year-Old Girl's School Science Project Was So Good, Now It's Patented!" Grape, October 14, 2015. https://grapee.jp/en/42763.

Johnson, Lee. "What Types of Metal Are Attracted to Magnets?" Sciencing website. Leaf Group Media. Updated June 7, 2018. https://sciencing.com/types-metal-attracted-magnets-5576017.html.

Kamiya, Asuka. "How a 12-Year-Old Girl Became One of the Youngest Japanese Patent Holders." Translated by Hiroko Kawano. Interviewed by Kayoko Shiomi. TEDxKyoto. Filmed November 2015. Uploaded by TEDx Talks, December 18, 2015. https://www.youtube.com/watch?v=0nNCXFT_Ots.

Shimbun, Chunichi. "Girl, 12, Lands Patent for Can-Separating Recycling Bin." *The Japan Times*, September 14, 2015. https://www.japantimes.co.jp/news/2015/09/14/national/girl-12-lands-patent-for-can-separating-recycling-bin.

———. "With Two Patents Under Her Belt, Aichi Junior High School Girl Looks to Help Other Inventive Kids." *The Japan Times*, November 13, 2017. https://www.japantimes.co.jp/news/2017/11/13/national/two-patents-belt-aichi-junior-high-school-girl-looks-help-inventive-kids/.

Gitanjali Rao

Rao, Gitanjali. "A Device to Detect Lead in Water by a 13-Year-Old Innovator." TEDxGateway. Filmed December 2018 in Mumbai, India. Uploaded by TEDx Talks, June 12, 2019. YouTube video, 11:03. https://www.youtube.com/watch?v=dn4SNdXqYBw.

Hall, Kelly, and Monica Hanson. "11-Year-Old Scientist Is Developing a Solution to Help Solve the Water Crisis in Flint, Michigan." 3M website. http://www.3m.com/3M/en_US/particles/all-articles/article-detail/~/clean-water-lead-detection-young-scientist-challenge/?storyid=e8e-a94e9-95b7-448a-bd74-79fbbb0a5960. Accessed January 16, 2022. (no longer available).

McIntosh, Amy. "Q&A: Gitanjali Rao—Time Magazine's 2020 Kid of the Year." *Water Quality Products Magazine*. January 21, 2022. Originally published as "Young Talent" in *Water Quality Products*, December 2017. https://www.wqpmag.com/qa/qa-gitanjali-rao-time-magazines-2020-kid-year.

Rao, Gitanjali. *A Young Innovator's Guide to STEM: 5 Steps to Problem Solving for Students, Educators, and Parents*. New York: Post Hill Press, 2021.

Sakas, Michael Elizabeth. "A 13-Year-Old Science Entrepreneur Wants to Bring Her Water Testing Device to Market." National Public Radio. *All Things Considered*. January 29, 2019. Mp3 audio, 3:54. https://www.npr.org/2019/01/29/687788715/a-13-year-old-science-entrepreneur-wants-to-bring-her-water-testing-device-to-ma.

Rao, Gitanjali. "Meet TIME's First-Ever Kid of the Year." Interviewed by Angelina Jolie. Transcribed by *Time* staff. *Time* magazine online. December 3, 2020. Video, 3:37. https://time.com/5916772/kid-of-the-year-2020/.

Xóchitl Guadalupe Cruz López

Cruz López, Xóchitl Guadalupe. Zoom interview. Conducted by Kailei Pew, June 2, 2021.

Cruz López, Xóchitl Guadalupe. "Niña Mexicana Gana un Premio de Ciencia Nuclear por Crear un Calentador Solar de Agua." Uploaded by Imagen Noticias, February 20, 2019. https://www.youtube.com/watch?v=OAs-B96vA2WU.

Rose, Shari. "Xóchitl Guadalupe Cruz López: How Child Inventor in Chiapas, Mexico Is Changing Lives." Blurred Bylines. February 21, 2021. https://

www.blurredbylines.com/articles/xochitl-guadalupe-cruz-lopez-child-inventor-chiapas-mx/.

Time for Kids. "7 Young Inventors Who See a Better Way." *Time*, Davos 2020 Issue. https://www.time.com/collection/davos-2020/5765632/young-inventors-changing-the-world/.

Wong, Alma Paola. "Ayudar a los Pobres, lo que Inspira a Xóchitl." Milenio Diarias. Más Culturas. Multimedios. March 6, 2018. https://www.milenio.com/cultura/ayudar-a-los-pobres-lo-que-inspira-a-xochitl.

López, Xóchitl Guadalupe Cruz. "Xóchitl Guadalupe Cruz López." Poder Cívico A. C. Uploaded by LaCiudaddelasIdeas. January 11, 2019. YouTube video. https://www.youtube.com/watch?v=_PaOvHgbAoU.

Agencia Informativa de Educación de México. "Xóchitl Guadalupe Cruz López es la Primera Niña en México que Recibe 'Reconocimiento ICN a la Mujer'." Uploaded by AIEDMX. May 9, 2018. YouTube video, 2:50. https://www.youtube.com/watch?v=f2MgYYwCwSk.

Inventions for Fun

Frank Epperson

Epperson, Frank. Frozen confectionery. US Patent US1505592A, filed July 19, 1924, and issued August 19, 1924. https://patents.google.com/patent/US1505592A/en.

Epperson, George. "My Pop Invented the Popsicle . . . By Accident!" *Reminisce* magazine, July/August 1992: 19. https://i.pinimg.com/originals/20/61/75/2061750060bc8f8de09b9c774acb7f1e.jpg.

Lang, Chris. Email interview. Conducted by Kailei Pew, July 3, 2021.

Pope, Shelby. "How an 11-Year-Old Boy Invented the Popsicle." National Public Radio. *The Salt: What's on Your Plate.* July 22, 2015. https://www.npr.org/sections/thesalt/2015/07/22/425294957/how-an-11-year-old-boy-invented-the-popsicle.

"Our Story: The Story Behind Popsicle® That Is Keeping You Cool Since 1905." Popsicle. https://www.popsicle.com/us/en/our-story.html.

Sharpe, Maggie. "What a Treat: Kathleen Epperson Recalls Her Grandfather's Popsicle Legacy." *Rossmoor News.* September 30, 2020. pp. 1A and 18A. https://rossmoornews-ca.newsmemory.com/?selDate=20200930&editionStart=Rossmoor%20News&goTo=A01&artid=3.

George Nissen

De Wyze, Jeannette. "The Man and the Kangaroo." Originally published in the *San Diego Reader*, August 13, 1998. Accessed via Brentwood Trampoline website. https://www.brentwoodtc.org/george_nissen.htm. (Confirmed in an interview with his daughter, Dian Nissen.)

"George Nissen: The Trampoline." Massachusetts Institute of Technology. https://lemelson.mit.edu/resources/george-nissen. Accessed March 15, 2021.

Nissen, Dian. Zoom interview. Conducted by Kailei Pew, March 8, 2021.

Nissen, George P. Tumbling device. US Patent US2370990A, filed June 4, 1941, and issued March 6, 1945. https://patents.google.com/patent /US2370990A/.

International Olympic Committee. "Tokyo 2020 Trampoline Gymnastics Results." Olympic Games Tokyo 2020. https://olympics.com/tokyo-2020/en /sports/trampoline-gymnastics/.

————. "Trampoline." Olympic Games. In association with International Gymnastics Federation. https://olympics.com/en/sports/trampoline-gymnastics/.

Peter Chilvers

Bornhoft, Simon. "50 Years of Windsurfing." *Windsurfing Magazine*. July 2009. pp. 73–75.

————. Email interview. Conducted by Kailei Pew, April 28, 2021.

Haggin, Patience. "A New Sport (and a New Legal Precedent)." *Time*. June 18, 2012. https://newsfeed.time.com/2012/06/19/7-amazing-teenage -inventors/slide/windsurfing-and-a-new-legal-precedent/.

UK Windsurfing Association. "Peter Chilvers." Hall of Fame. https://uk windsurfing.com/hall-of-fame/peter-chilvers/.

"UKWA Hall of Fame." *Boards Windsurfing Magazine*. April 19, 2013. https:// boards.co.uk/news/ukwa-hall-of-fame.html.

Chilvers, Peter. "windsurf from one show." The One Show. Uploaded by bicycleman88, June 10, 2009. YouTube video, 4:11. https://www.youtube .com/watch?v=CQZLKGZ6vgk.

Hridayeshwar Singh Bhati

Bhati, Hridayeshwar Singh. "Dhoni Gave Award to Real Life Hero Hridayeshwar Singh Bhati." Edited by Mahesh Jagadappa. Viral Bollywood. Uploaded by Viralbollywood, November 15, 2014. YouTube video, 9:32. https://www.youtube.com/watch?v=_2lFSxCgTmk.

Ability Foundation & CavinKareIndia. "National Award for Disable Hero Won by Hridayeshwar Singh Bhati, Youngest Patent Holder of India." 11th CavinKare National Ability Award. Filmed March 9, 2013 at Sir Mutha Concert Hall, Chennai, India. Uploaded by Sarowersingh Bhati, January 24, 2015. YouTube video, 12/l08. https://www.youtube.com /watch?v=4HPU8NPk1v8.

Pareek, Rakshita. "Can't Move but Mind Can Run." *First India.* January 13, 2020, Vol. 1 Issue 218, p. 4.

Press Trust of India. *Jaipur Teen Becomes World's Youngest Differently-Abled Patent Holder.* NDTV.com, November 21, 2019. https://www.ndtv .com/india-news/jaipur-teen-hridayeshwar-singh-bhati-becomes-worlds -youngest-differently-abled-patent-holder-2136265.

Singh, Ajay. "Youngest Patent Holder on Wheelchair." *The Times of India.* March 30, 2012. https://timesofindia.indiatimes.com/city/jaipur /youngest-patent-holder-on-wheelchair/articleshow/12463291.cms.

Singh Bhati, Hridayeshwar. Circular Chess. India patent 252967 issued August 19, 2013.

———. Facebook messenger interview. Conducted by Kailei Pew, January 23–26, 2021.

Bhati, Sarowersingh. "Six Players Circular Chess Invented by Youngest Patent Holder of India & Youngest Disabled Patent Holder." Uploaded by Sarowersingh Bhati, December 11, 2014. YouTube video, 7:50. https:// www.youtube.com/watch?v=9uNAmBtxkBk.

Tripp Phillips

Berger, Sarah. "'Shark Tank' Premiere: Kevin O'Leary Gave a 12-Year-Old $80,000 for This Genius Company." CNBC Make It, October 8, 2018. https://www.cnbc.com/2018/10/08/shark-tank-premiere-kevin-oleary -gave-a-12-year-old-80000.html.

Phillips, Tripp. Email interview. Conducted by Kailei Pew, January 28, 2021.

———. "How This 13 Year Old Made It On Shark Tank and Did $500K in Sales." Starter Story. February 14, 2019. https://www.starterstory.com /stories/how-this-13-year-old-made-it-on-shark-tank-and-did-500k-in -sales.

———. "Interview Tripp Phillips Creator of Le Glue." Uploaded by Corriente Latina, February 27, 2019. YouTube video, 3:54. https://www.youtube .com/watch?v=x3VNdCwqEpg.

Rock, Mariah. "Dalton Teen Invents Glue that Holds Building Blocks To- gether and Dissolves in Water." ABC News Channel 9. November 1, 2019. https://newschannel9.com/features/made-in-our-hometown/glue -that-keeps-building-blocks-together-dissolves-in-water-a-13-year-olds -invention.

Le-Glue. "The Story Behind Le-Glue." About Us. https://www.le-glue.com /about/. Accessed February 26, 2021.

Jordan Reeves

Born Just Right. "Our Mission." https://www.bornjustright.org/. Accessed March 20, 2021.

Henderson, Jalyn. "Project Unicorn: The Glitter Shooting Prosthetic Arm." ABC 7 Chicago, March 22, 2019. https://abc7chicago.com/jordan -reeves-jen-lee-project-unicorn-born-just-right/5210907/.

Krasavage, Nicole. "A Girl and Her Glitter-Shooting Prosthetic: 'You Can Do Anything,'" CNN Health. February 13, 2017. https://www.cnn.com /2017/02/13/health/jordan-reeves-born-just-right-limb-difference -profile/index.html.

Lowin, Rebekah. "This 10-Year-Old Girl Designed Her Own Prosthetic Arm— And It Shoots Sparkles!" *Today*, March 31, 2016. https://www.today.com /news/10-year-old-girl-designed-her-own-prosthetic-arm-it-t83451.

Reeves, Jordan. Project Unicorn website. Born Just Right. 2021. https:// jordanreeves.com/project-unicorn.

Reeves, Jen Lee. "Keeping Up with Project Unicorn." Born Just Right. March 28, 2016. https://www.bornjustright.org/keeping-up-with-project -unicorn/.

Reeves, Jordan. *Born Just Right*. New York: Aladdin, 2019, p. 143.

Reeves, Jordan, and Jen Reeves. "Born Just Right: Project Unicorn at SXSW."

Uploaded by AMI: Accessible Media Inc. August 30, 2018. https://www
.youtube.com/watch?v=jv2pjbtoUo8.

"Teen Turns Prosthetic Arm into Glitter-Shooting Unicorn Horn." WGN
News's *Evening News*. Uploaded by WGN News, March 27, 2019. YouTube
video, 2:56. https://www.youtube.com/watch?v=Tf91U06GII8&t=58s.

"TinkerStar: Jordan Reeves, Creator of Project Unicorn." Uploaded by Autodesk Tinkercad, March 1, 2017. https://www.youtube.com/watch?
v=7gBP2BbalNM.

Alex Butler

Taco vs Burrito Team. "About Us." Taco vs Burrito website. https://tacovs
burrito.com/pages/about-us.

Busch, Howie. "So Easy, a 7-Year-Old Can Do It." *Inventors Digest*, February 27, 2020. https://www.inventorsdigest.com/articles/so-easy-a-7
-year-old-can-do-it/.

Butler, Alex, and Leslie Pierson. Zoom interview. Conducted by Kailei Pew,
April 10, 2021.

Grygiel, JiaYing. "Meet the Seattle kid who invented the $1 million-grossing
Taco vs Burrito game when he was 7." *The Seattle Times*. Updated
May 28, 2020. https://www.seattletimes.com/life/meet-the-seattle-kid
-who-invented-a-1-million-grossing-card-game/.

———. "Seattle Boy Invented the Hot-Selling Family Game Taco vs Burrito."
Seattle's Child. Updated September 11, 2020. https://www.seattles
child.com/seattle-boy-invented-the-family-game-taco-vs-burrito/.

Hot Taco Enterprises. "Taco vs. Burrito: A Crazy Fun Game Created by a 7
Year Old." Kickstarter campaign website. Author access date: March
8, 2021. https://www.kickstarter.com/projects/hottaco/taco-vs-burrito.

Cornelius, Jeff. "How to Play Taco Vs Burrito." Uploaded by Board and Brew
Games, September 7, 2018. https://www.youtube.com/watch?v=mz
trM823xYc.

ACKNOWLEDGMENTS

It's hard to believe that I'm writing this right now. There were many times when I didn't think I would ever make it to this point. To be here feels like an absolute dream. But a dream that would not have been possible without the incredible support of those around me. How very grateful I am for the many, *many* people who made this book possible.

First, to Brad, for being the most supportive husband on the planet and believing in me, even when I didn't believe in myself. For reading countless excerpts and helping me feel like I really could do this. For wiping my tears when I was convinced I could *not*. For picking up all the chocolate peanut butter ice cream I requested. And for holding down the fort when I was researching, interviewing, and writing my heart out. I love you more than words can say, and I am so grateful we have each other.

Thank you to my beautiful children for being my biggest fans and celebrating me on this journey. I know there were times when you had to have incredible patience, and I am so grateful. Thank you for inspiring this entire book with your boundless creativity and confidence. Thank you for making life such a joy. From snuggling up with a good book, to playing a board game or having an epic dance party, our time together is the best. I love you so much. My favorite role will always be that of being "Mommy."

To Mom and Dad for being the greatest parents a girl could ask for. Thank you for cheering me on, encouraging me when it got hard, and for babysitting many times while I wrote. It means the world to me that you have always supported my dreams and taught me that I can do and be anything I want to be. I love you both so much.

Thank you to my Grandma Jo for letting me tell you every detail of this book on our Tuesday visits. Those weekly chats are so special to me and I can't tell you enough how much I enjoy them. You've always been there for me and I am so very grateful. Grandpa sure would have been proud, wouldn't he?

Thank you to the rest of my family. My in-laws, siblings, aunts, uncles, cousins, nieces, and nephews. Thank you for letting me talk your ears off about books, for being such big supporters, and for always lifting me up. I have the greatest family.

To Emily Forney, agent extraordinaire, thank you for making my dreams come true! For getting this and all of my books into the right hands, for listening to my teary phone calls, for screaming with me over our successes, and for putting up with entirely too many text messages, thank you. You are the absolute greatest and I truly could not ask for a better partner on this wild journey.

A huge thank-you to Holly West for seeing in this book more than I saw myself. For pushing me to write it in a way that I didn't even know I was capable of. For encouraging me, being patient with me, and helping me along this new middle grade journey, thank you. It has truly been an honor to work with you and learn from you. This book would not be even a fraction of what it is if it wasn't for you.

To Starr Baer, Maria Vlasak, Kim Waymer, L. Whitt, and everyone else on the MacKids team, a huge thank you. I had no idea how many hands go into making a book before starting this process, and I am so grateful to each and every one of you for all of your hard work and commitment to this project.

To Shannon Wright, thank you so much for collaborating with me on this project. It was an absolute dream to work with you. To say I was fan-girling when you agreed to the project would be an understatement. You are so very talented, and I feel beyond blessed to have partnered with you.

To Hollie, Shereen, and Tiffany, thank you for being such a great group of critique partners and lifelong friends. Thank you for reading this one from the very first (very bad) draft through today. Thank you for letting me cry in our group chats and for encouraging me to keep pressing forward always. I love that we are on this journey together.

Thank you to the MG Dreamers, Katie, Jordan, Kaye, Shondra, and Tracy. I am so grateful that you came together in a time when I truly needed you. Thank you for helping me learn how to go beyond picture books and into middle grade territory. Your expertise and advice were invaluable.

To my agent sibling family, I adore you all. Your chats and support have meant the world to me. I feel so blessed to be grouped with such an awesome bunch of creators. Emily really knows how to pick them!

To Michelle Mohrweis for beta reading early drafts, providing so much positivity and encouragement when I was down, and for helping me understand robotics. Thank you!

Thank you to Benjamin Russell and Anthony Millett for giving me multiple lessons on logic gates and helping me understand at my very beginner's level.

The *biggest* thank-you I can muster to the amazing kid inventors, family members, and friends who I was able to interview for this book. Thank you for taking time to meet with me via Zoom, email, or instant messaging and for responding to my *many* follow up questions. Karoli Hindriks, Norm Goldstein, Sofia Overton, Lily Born, Maria Vitória Valoto, Bishop Curry V and family, Collin Kobayashi with 3D Innovations, Fatima Al Kaabi, Ann Makosinski and Heidi Kleinmaus, Samaira Mehta, Yuma Soerianto, Ken Lou Castillo, Xóchitl Guadalupe Cruz López, Chris Lang, Dian Nissen, Simon Bornhoft with Windwise, Hridayeshwar Singh Bhati, Tripp Phillips, Alex Butler, Leslie Pierson, Mary Couzin with the People of Play Young Inventor Challenge, Ken Torisky at National Inventors Hall of Fame, Mark Leschinsky, Ehan Kamat, Rachel Zimmerman Brachman, and Adia Bulawa. Your stories were so inspirational, and meeting with you was the best part about making this book.

And finally, to you, dear reader. Thank you for taking the time to learn about each of these incredible kid inventors. I feel so happy and grateful that I was able to share their stories with you all. I hope you feel inspired to create, innovate, and build something new. I hope you know that you can do anything you set your mind to. And I hope you know that you are never too young to make a difference.

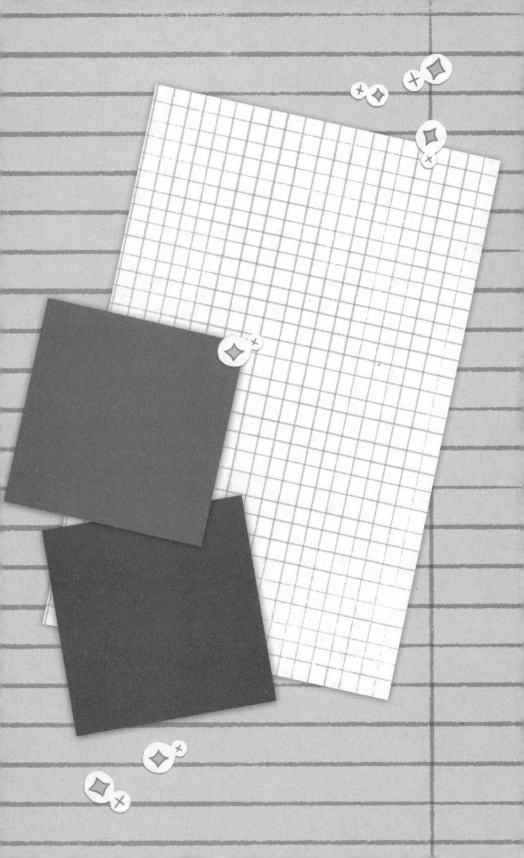

Thank you for reading this Feiwel & Friends book. The friends who made **KID-VENTORS** possible are:

Jean Feiwel, Publisher
Liz Szabla, VP, Associate Publisher
Rich Deas, Senior Creative Director
Holly West, Senior Editor
Anna Roberto, Senior Editor
Kat Brzozowski, Senior Editor
Dawn Ryan, Executive Managing Editor
Kim Waymer, Senior Production Manager
Emily Settle, Editor
Rachel Diebel, Editor
Foyinsi Adegbonmire, Associate Editor
Brittany Groves, Assistant Editor
L. Whitt, Designer
Starr Baer, Production Editor

Follow us on Facebook or visit us online at mackids.com.
Our books are friends for life.